CRUSOES AND CASTAWAYS

True Stories of Survival & Solitude

CRUSOES AND CASTAWAYS

True Stories of Survival & Solitude

STANLEY ROGERS

With an Introduction by
JOHN HARLAND

DOVER PUBLICATIONS, INC.
Mineola, New York

Bibliographical Note

This Dover edition, first published in 2011, is an unabridged republication of
the work originally published in 1932 by George G. Harrap & Co., London. The
only significant alteration consists in moving the map that originally appeared as
an endpaper to pages 10 and 11. Also, a new Introduction has been provided by
John Harland specially for this Dover edition.

Library of Congress Cataloging-in-Publication Data

Rogers, Stanley, 1888–1961
    Crusoes and castaways / Stanley Rogers ; illustrated by the author.
       p. cm.
    Originally published: London : G. G. Harrap, 1932.
    Includes index.
    ISBN-13: 978-0-486-47897-5
    ISBN-10: 0-486-47897-1
    1. Shipwrecks. 2. Adventure and adventurers. I. Title.

G525.R583 2011
910.45'20922—dc22

2011003429

Manufactured in the United States by Courier Corporation
47897101
www.doverpublications.com

INTRODUCTION TO THE DOVER EDITION

It is a great pleasure to introduce a new generation of readers to the work of Stanley Reginald Harold Rogers (1888 – 1961). The author of *Crusoes and Castaways* was born in the state of Washington, but went overseas to study art at Goldsmiths College, London. As things turned out, he was to remain in England until the end of World War II, when he moved to New York and lived there for the rest of his life. Starting in the late twenties, he authored and illustrated over fifty books for children and adults, many of them, like this one, with a maritime theme. Books in this category include *Sea Lore, Tales of the Fore-and-Aft, Ships and Sailors, The Pacific, The Atlantic,* and *The Indian Ocean.* An accomplished painter, he was one of the founding members of the Royal Society of Marine Artists, and a master of the pen-and-ink sketch. His style is easily recognizable … nice variety and economy of line, with considerable use of massed blacks and silhouette. His wife Frances, *née* Woodhouse, whom he met at art school, also achieved popular success as an author and illustrator of children's books, under the name Franke Rogers, and their son Cedric Rogers was to carry on the family tradition as writer and illustrator of *Sailing Ships,* and several popular works on geology.

The word *castaway* instantly evokes in everybody's mind the image of Robinson Crusoe, clad in goatskin clothes and conical cap, and carrying his musket and umbrella, so it is perfectly appropriate that the first part of the book starts off with famous fictional castaways, rather than real ones. Scholars consider Defoe's *Robinson Crusoe* to be the first English novel, but when first published in 1719, it purported to be an authentic account of the sufferings of a real shipwrecked seafarer. Its full title was

1

CRUSOES AND CASTAWAYS

The Life and Strange Surprizing Adventures of Robinson Crusoe of York, Mariner: Who lived Eight and Twenty Years, all alone in an un-inhabited Island on the coast of America, near the Mouth of the Great River of Oroonoque; Having been cast on Shore by Shipwreck, wherein all the Men perished but himself. With An Account how he was at last as strangely deliver'd by Pyrates. Written by Himself. From the opening sentence: "I was born in the year 1632, in the city of York, of a good family, though not of that country, my father being a foreigner of Bremen, who settled first at Hull", through the painstakingly catalogued lists of salvaged items: "I found two or three bags full of nails and spikes, a great screw-jack, a dozen or two of hatchets, and above all, that most useful thing called a grindstone", the account was rich in detail and thoroughly convincing. No wonder all but the most skeptical initially accepted it as the real article. Alexander Selkirk, to whom we will return below, believed that he was the single immediate wellspring and origin of *Robinson Crusoe*, and this opinion is indeed the generally accepted opinion. However, was this really the case? In 1712, his story was published anonymously in a pamphlet entitled *Providence Display'd, or The Remarkable Adventures of one Mr. Alexander Selkirk*, and is discussed in *A Cruising Voyage Around the World*, written by his rescuer, Captain Woodes Rogers. In addition, Essayist Richard Steele had written up his conversation with Selkirk in the magazine *The Englishman*, and in any case, the story was very well known, and Defoe may even have met the Scottish sailor personally. However, he is by no means the only possible literary ancestor. Timothy Severin in *The Search for Robinson Crusoe* (2002), makes a compelling argument for the *Relation of the Great Suffering and Strange Adventures of Henry Pitman, Surgeon to the late Duke of Monmouth* published in 1689, as being the real nucleus of the idea. Pitman and Defoe almost certainly knew each other, both having been implicated in the Monmouth Rebellion, and sharing the same publisher. Moreover, Salt Tortuga the uninhabited island, upon which Pitman was marooned lies northeast of Venezuela and at a similar latitude to Crusoe's island, and hence is an infinitely better geographic fit than the Islands of Juan Fernandez, on the other side of the equator and the South American continent. David Fausett the author of *The Strange Surprizing Sources of Robinson Crusoe* argues that Hendrik Smeek's *Beschryvinge van het Magtig Koningryk van Krinke Kesmes (An account of the mighty kingdom of Krisme Kesmes),* published in 1708 was a key source. Other possible claimants have been put forward, but this is the stuff of academic dissertations. Defoe may well have read and been influenced by any or all these, but like all novelists he was entitled to draw on his background and reading, and *Robinson Crusoe* remains his work, and his alone, and unquestionably worthy of its place as an icon of English literature.

Travels into Several Remote Nations of the World. In Four Parts. By Lemuel Gulliver, first a Surgeon and then a Captain of Several Ships, was published anonymously in 1726. As with Crusoe, it purported to be a real travel story, even featuring a portrait of Gulliver, and became a roaring success, although, or partly because, it was in reality a vitriolic political satire. The much shortened and bowdlerized versions available today concentrate on the first of Lemuel Gulliver's four voyages, the one to Lilliput. Swift was perhaps inspired to write Gulliver because of the immense popular success of Crusoe, but the two works are quite unalike and there was no love lost between the two authors. Swift refers to Defoe as "that fellow that was pilloried, I have forgot his name." (Defoe had been sentenced to the pillory because his pamphlet, *The Shortest Way with Dissenters,* ruthlessly satirized the Anglican Church), and Defoe described Swift as "Dr S--- the copper farthing dean, who can preach and read prayers in the morning, write bawdy in the afternoon, and profanity at night."

Robinson Crusoe engendered a whole new fictional genre, which became especially popular in Germany, where such works were collectively known as *Robinsonaden.* Perhaps the category could usefully be restricted to tales that describe survival against all odds on a desert island, and thus include R. M. Ballantyne's *Coral Island,* Frederick Marryat's *Masterman Ready*, together

3

with more recent items like Robert A Heinlein's science-fiction *Tunnel in the Sky* (1955) and the film *Cast Away* starring Tom Hanks (2000). It would exclude Johann Wyss's *The Swiss Family Robinson* because the heroes are shipwrecked upon a veritable Eden, and Gulliver because of its satiric intent and the absence of the survivalist element.

Over the years, many readers have been bothered by the title *Swiss Family Robinson. Der Schweizerischer Robinson* would better be translated as *The Swiss Robinson Crusoes*, making it clear that we are not talking about the family name, but about their predicament. Several English translations have appeared, the best known of which is that by W. H. G. Kingston (1879). Although clearly based on *Crusoe*, in Johann Wyss's version, a beneficent nature provides for the castaways' every need and convenience, and the book ends with several of the main characters deciding to remain on the island of "New Switzerland", rather than return to civilization. Father, who is a rather irritating know-it-all, instructs the children in the proper use of each opportune natural discovery, learning the value of frugality, cooperation and Christian virtue as they do so. All these authors are not just telling a story, but advancing their own particular political and religious views. Defoe considered his book an allegory for his own spiritual development, and Wyss, Marryat and Ballantyne, all wrote to edify their young readers as well as entertain them. Marryat is said to have written *Masterman Ready* for his own children because he was thoroughly irritated at the countless inaccuracies and inconsistencies in the Swiss story.

Then we move on to a variety of real life stories, starting with that of Alexander Selkirk. In 1704, following a quarrel with the captain of the *Cinque Ports*, of which he was sailing master, he was put ashore at his own request on the Isla Más-a-Tierra, easternmost of the Juan Fernandez islands, and was to remain there for four years, until rescued by Woodes Rogers in the privateer *Duke*. His survival demanded great determination and ingenuity, but later research has established that he was far from a model character.

4

INTRODUCTION TO THE DOVER EDITION

Perhaps because of Crusoe, we imagine people being cast ashore on islands with tropical climates, but not all victims of shipwreck were so lucky. Here you will find the harrowing tale of the stranded English whalers who were cast ashore in Greenland winter in 1630, and the Russians who faced bitter cold and starvation on East Spitsbergen from 1743 to 1749.

Rogers provides at least one example of what we might call voluntary crusoehood. In 1871 two young Prussians, Gustav and Friedrich Stoltenhoff, persuaded the captain of a whaler to land them on uninhabited Inaccessible Island near Tristan da Cunha, where they planned to farm. After much privation and many hardships they were taken off by HMS *Challenger* two years later.

Not all shipwreck stories have a happy ending. The ship referred to on page 225 was the *Tamaris* of Bordeaux which was wrecked on one of the Crozet Islands in the Southern Indian Ocean. The crew tried to communicate with the outside world by capturing a great petrel, and banding its leg with a strip of tin reading: "13 shipwrecked sailors are on the Crozets, 4 August 1887." Remarkably, the message was recovered in Western Australia some weeks later, but by the time a rescue mission was organized, the castaways had run out of food and sailed for another island in the ship's boat, with their fate remaining unknown. In other chapters we discover that not all shipwrecked sailors suffer their fate in total wretchedness. In 1818 the East-Indiaman *Cabalva* was wrecked on a reef off Cargados Garayos near Mauritius, but the castaways were sustained by salvaged casks of ale and wine, and allegedly some of them never drew a sober breath during their three week sojourn on "Beer Island."

It is my hope that this Dover edition of *Crusoes and Castaways* will spur renewed interest in the works of Stanley Rogers and enthrall a whole new generation of readers.

John Harland
August, 2010

FOREWORD

How sweet, how passing sweet, is solitude;
But grant me still a friend in my retreat,
Whom I may whisper—solitude is sweet.
WILLIAM COWPER, *Retirement*

TO say that man is a gregarious animal is merely to emphasize the obvious. Most of us prefer to be within reach of our fellow-men, however roundly we may curse them at times. Few are born with the hermit instinct; the rest of us shudder at the very thought of such self-immolation, and gather closer round the fires of humanity, leaving the saints to their cold and gloomy heights. But while the life of a lighthouse-keeper, or, better still, that of a castaway on some lonely islet, may not in any sense appeal to us, we, with an almost sadistic pleasure, love reading of the experiences of these involuntary hermits. Let the wind howl in the chimney how it may, before a cheerful fire and settled in a deep armchair we find the journal of Robinson Crusoe a most satisfying entertainment.

There is no denying that we get more thrill out of adversity than ease. Is not the diary of a poor traveller more entertaining than the diary of a rich traveller? What worth-while adventures can the pampered saloon passenger get in a floating hotel, with its Ritz-Carlton grills and Louis Quinze suites? The easy lot of the Swiss Family Robinson is as tepid water compared with the sparkling wine of Crusoe's adversities.

At heart we are primitive when it comes to a tale of adventure. Be we never so squeamish, when our castaways piously confess that they resorted to cannibalism, sacrificing one to save the many, we are not so shocked as we imagine. It is said that during the Great War nice old ladies sat over their knitting talking like cannibals. And what mother was not proud of her son for the notches on the stock of his

7

rifle? When the primitive is aroused we quickly shed the ideals of civilization. Let these tales be bowdlerized of their misery and suffering, and who would read them? Hence I have set them down as I have found them, neither adding nor deleting. They are real-life episodes, and need no exaggerations to give them dramatic value. Indeed, were it not contrary to my own interest, which is to tempt the reader to read this book, I would recommend him to go to the original sources, where he would find the simple records of these adventures honestly set down by their protagonists while the matter was still green in their memories. They had no thought of exploiting their misfortunes. It was only later, perhaps, when they returned destitute to civilization, that they were made to realize that their story was worth the telling. Alexander Selkirk returned a quiet, thoughtful fellow, not entirely pleased to be back in bumbledom, and was only with difficulty and through the importunings of Sir Richard Steele persuaded to make his tale generally known.

How the shades of these Crusoes might compare notes were they to read this collection! I see Selkirk smiling indulgently on the two German youths who, within living memory, attempted to emulate his adventures on an island in the South Atlantic, and Lieutenant Byron conning, with the eye of an expert in starvation, the account of the tribulations of the *Delphine's* people on the same coast seventy-three years later, and thinking, no doubt, how lightly they fared compared with his own historic wretchedness. I hope, if their ghosts are looking over my shoulder, that they find nothing here but what is true, that they have no complaints that justice is not done them, and that their adventures have not lost too much of their dignity in translation.

Shades of all castaways, I hail you with gratitude for the material for this book!

S. R. H. R.

London
1932

CONTENTS

9

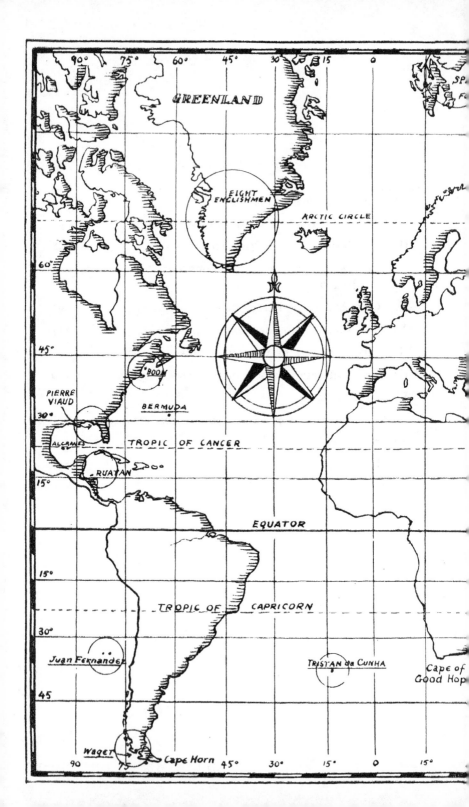

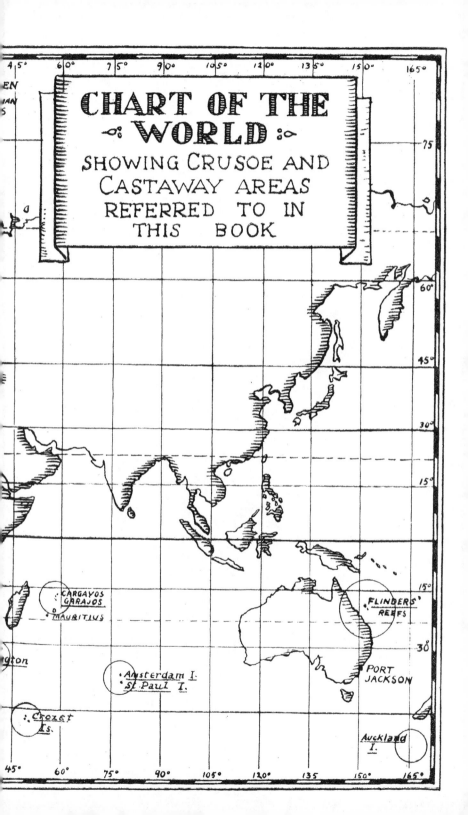

CHART OF THE ∽: WORLD :∽
SHOWING CRUSOE AND CASTAWAY AREAS REFERRED TO IN THIS BOOK

CHAPTER I

Divers Crusoes of Fiction

O N the 25th of April, in the year 1719, there appeared
in London a book that was destined to set a fashion
in the art of fiction narrative that has endured to
this day, and may survive on into the dim mists of futurity,
until gregarious man becomes too intellectually dehumanized
to care longer for mental pabulum of such a crude and
unsophisticated *genre*. I refer to the Crusoe narrative—
a tale of an exile, or exiles, on a desert island, a tale which
has had a thousand imitators since Daniel Defoe, of Stoke
Newington, launched his astonishing book on an appre-
ciative world. The central idea has always been the same,
however much it has been smothered in extraneous inven-
tion. There is always a desert or desolate shore or island
and a shipwrecked or marooned hero, who spends an un-
conscionable long time exiled from the bumbledom called
civilization. Sometimes our protagonist is accompanied by
others; sometimes he meets fabulous monsters or has fantastic experiences; but always there is the privation and
loneliness attendant upon exile in the desert places of the
earth. In the earlier forms it was common to introduce
fantastic creatures and make the hero perform impossible
feats and suffer incredible privation of body; in the latest
a plot is introduced. The island paradise is disturbed by
the presence of Eve, or perhaps two Eves and one Adam,

or two Adams and one Eve. We have progressed far since the pious *naïveté* of poor old Robinson Crusoe.

The Hollywood Movie Moguls have found it a profitable source of revenue by serving it up with a heroine washed ashore immaculate, and with a peace-disturbing aura of sex appeal. Her father's luxury yacht effects a timely rescue,

A HEROINE WASHED ASHORE

after some judicious roughing it on a palm-fringed beach, and every one lives happily ever after. The unreality of some of these Californian castaway tales, with their excessive sentimentality, makes Barrie's sentimental play, *The Admirable Crichton*, almost austere in comparison. Some years ago Hollywood filmed *The Admirable Crichton*, entirely emasculating it of its original virility, and, I believe, improving its title—giving it something 'snappy.' In short, they made the picture a travesty of the play, just as they treated the immortal *Moby Dick*, calling it *The Sea Beast* and giving it a sentimental and happy ending, with love and a rose-grown cottage.

To return to the prototype of this venerable line of castaway narratives. It first appeared without the actual author's name,[1] a fact which lent actuality to the story told by the mysterious mariner named Robinson Crusoe. The title-page of the first edition read as follows:

THE
LIFE
and
STRANGE SURPRIZING
ADVENTURES
of
ROBINSON CRUSOE
Of *YORK*, Mariner:

Who lived Eight and Twenty Years,
all alone in an un-inhabited Island on the
COAST OF AMERICA, near the Mouth of
the Great River of OROONOQUE;

Having been cast on Shore by Shipwreck, wherein all the Men perished but himself.

With
An Account how he was at last as strangely
deliver'd by PYRATES.

———

Written by Himself.

LONDON:

Printed for W. Taylor at the *Ship* in *Pater-
Noster-Row*, MDCCXIX.

---

[1] The authorship has been attributed to others besides Defoe, but on such flimsy evidence that it may be disregarded.

The 1722 edition contained in the editor's preface this statement:

> The Editor believes the Thing to be a just History of Facts; neither is there any Appearance of Fiction in it: and however Thinks, because all such Things are disputed, that the Improvement of it, as well to the Diversion, as to the Instruction of the

> Reader, will be the same; and as such, he thinks, without farther Compliment to the World, he does them a great service in Publication.

It quickly appeared in several editions in England,[1] and was widely pirated, a fact which gives our latter-day bibliophiles no little entertainment. The original was reprinted serially in *Heathcote's Intelligencer*, and is probably the first authentic instance of narrative fiction being published in this form—the world's first serial. So popular became the tale that it was not long before it was being translated into a number of European languages. Then came the legions of imitators, the best known of which is probably *The Swiss Family Robinson*, an artificial tale written for

[1] The first four editions appeared in as many months.

young people, of which more presently. In 1720 appeared
a sequel to *Robinson Crusoe*, called *Serious Reflections*, a work
that has not the spontaneity and genius of the former, and
is now no longer read. It was patently an excuse, a mouth-
piece for Defoe's own sentiments on religion and life.

That Defoe got his inspiration from
Dampier's *New Voyage Round the World*,
and particularly from a personal meeting with Alexander Selkirk at the house
of a mutual friend, Mrs Damaris Daniel,
in Bristol, is well known. Defoe is
supposed to have received from Selkirk
all the latter's notes concerning his
memorable exile on Juan Fernandez. If
this be true was there ever a better
instance of the "noble plagiarist"?

It may perhaps be regrettable that
half the classics in literature have been
abridged for children. Regrettable because, having read in our youth the
epitomized (and bowdlerized) versions,
we have no appetite to read the richer
originals later. How many people have
read the complete *Gulliver*, or *Crusoe*,
or the *Odyssey*? What company of sober
adults could take Robinson Crusoe seriously? Was he not left behind at ado-
lescence, along with Sindbad the Sailor
and the Swiss Family Robinson? Yet

ROBINSON CRUSOE
As depicted in the
1722 edition.

read him and be astonished at the substance in him. He is
as real a creature as ever lived; indeed, he is one of us. He
thought and acted just as a modern man would have done in
his place. There is hardly a false note in the entire book.
Even his extreme unmodern piety becomes understandable
when we begin to realize the unspeakable loneliness of
his condition.

And now, having deplored the habit of abridging the classics, I am going to fall into the same error with a brief epitome of the story. But the very title of the present book cries out for some reference to Defoe's masterpiece.

Robinson Crusoe, born in the famous city of York in the year 1632, owed his curious name to the happy mating of the maternal and paternal family names: Robinson from his mother's side (she was an Englishwoman), and Crusoe an Anglicized version of Kreutznaer, his own proper surname, for his father was a German from the port of Bremen, long since domiciled in England *via* the port of Hull. Fortunately for the world, Crusoe grew up to be a more than usually restless youth, and nothing but going to sea would satisfy him. So for eight years he sailed deep waters, making many long and adventurous voyages, and gaining the resourcefulness and knowledge that was to stand him in such good stead during his unparalleled experience on his famous island. The most noteworthy of his early adventures was his capture by a Salee rover and escape after two years as a slave in the hands of the Moors. Putting out to sea in a boat stolen from his master, he was picked up by friendly Spaniards and taken to Brazil, where for a while he lived as a planter. It was from there that he embarked on the voyage which left him shipwrecked without a human companion on a 'desolate' isle off the coast of Guinea, and incidentally on the opposite side of the South American continent to that of Alexander Selkirk's island—Juan Fernandez. The description of every incident, the local colour, and the technical details are generally beyond reproach. The plausibility of the tale is remarkable. Defoe displays a knowledge of the sea and ships, of topography, natural history, navigation, meteorology, and foreign customs which must have been outside the range of his own experience. Nor did he fall into the contemporary errors of gross anachronisms. And, together with this range of knowledge, he possessed the indefinable touch of the artist whose art is in fooling his audience.

The story was a magnificent hoax—until the truth came out, and doubtless half his readers remained until the end of their lives reluctant to believe that Crusoe never really existed. He was altogether too much of flesh and blood to be a creature of the imagination. Throughout the book one comes across those trifling things that happen only in real life—or in the mind of a great artist. Speaking of the embarkation for what turned out to be the disastrous last voyage, he said:

> But I hurried on, and obeyed blindly the dictates of my fancy rather than my reason. And accordingly, the ship being fitted out and the cargo furnished, and all things done as by agreement by my partners in the voyage, I went on board in an evil hour, the first of September, 1659, being the same day eight year that I went from my father at Hull in order to act the rebel to their authority and the fool to my own interest.

The ship, a vessel of 120 tons, carried fourteen men besides the captain, his boy, and Crusoe himself. That, with the sole exception of Crusoe, all these people should have perished is not stretching probability in the least. Similar cases have occurred at sea on several well-authenticated occasions. He and his companions stood out from the port of St Salvador, in Brazil, on what was intended to be a trading voyage—which included the buying of slaves—to the coast of Guinea. About two weeks later they ran into bad weather somewhere, as near as they could tell, in 12° 18' North latitude—weather which was to be their undoing. The ship grounded on a sandbank, and in the breaking seas her people took to the boat in an attempt to gain the shore. How the boat capsized and how Crusoe, half-drowned, got ashore is described with a verisimilitude that is uncanny. No incident in the chapters of castaways which follow could be more convincing than this simply told description of his coming to his island. Defoe does not insult the intelligence with the cheap tricks of the second-rate artist. As Crusoe is beaten ashore, the lone survivor of his company, we find ourselves sharing his despair.

> I began to look round me to see what kind of place I was in, and what was next to be done, and I soon found my comforts abate, and that in a word I had a dreadful deliverance; for I was wet, had no clothes to shift me, not anything to eat or drink to comfort me, neither did I see any prospect before me but that of perishing with hunger, or being devoured by wild beasts; and that which was particularly afflicting to me was, that I had no weapon either to hunt and kill any creature, for my sustenance, or to defend myself against any other creature that might desire to kill me for theirs. . . . Night coming upon me, I began with a heavy heart to consider what would be my lot if there were any ravenous beasts in that country, seeing that at night they always come abroad for their prey.

The first night was spent in a tree against possible attacks by "ravenous beasts," and the next day, being still alive, the wretched castaway swam out to the wreck, which lay fast on a bank a quarter of a mile from the shore at low water. How alone he contrived to build a raft and get some stores ashore is a reasoned piece of fiction that leaves nothing to be desired by the captious. Crusoe describes in detail how he got the stores ashore, and, of course, gives us an inventory of everything. The business was by no means plain sailing.

> As I imagined, so it was; there appeared before me a little opening of the land, and I found a strong current of the tide set into it; so I guided my raft as well as I could to keep in the middle of the stream. But here I had like to have suffered a second shipwreck, which, if I had, I think verily would have broke my heart; for, knowing nothing of the coast, my raft ran aground at one end of it upon a shoal, and not being aground at the other end, it wanted but a little that my cargo had slipped off towards the end that was afloat, and so fallen into the water. I did my utmost by setting my back against the chests to keep them in their places, but

could not thrust off the raft with all my strength, neither durst I stir from the posture I was in, but holding up the chests with all my might, stood in that manner near half an hour, in which time the rising of the water brought me a little more upon a level; and a little after, the water still rising, my raft floated again, and I thrust her off with the oar I had into the channel, and then driving up higher, I at length found myself in the mouth of a little river, with land on both sides, and a strong current or tide running up. . . .

At length I spied a little cove on the right shore of the creek, to which, with great pain, and difficulty, I guided my raft, and at last got so near as that, reaching ground with my oar, I could thrust her directly in; but here I had like to have dipped all my cargo into the sea again; for that shore lying pretty steep, that is to say, sloping, there was no place to land but where one end of my float if it run on shore, would lie so high and the other sink lower, as before, that it would endanger my cargo again.

However, he surmounted the difficulty by holding the raft close to the shore until the tide coming in floated it higher up the beach, where there was a flat piece of sand now submerged. Over this he moored the raft by thrusting oars into the sand, and when the tide ebbed the whole affair, raft and cargo, settled on hard ground. The next few days were too much occupied with getting food and stores ashore for repining, but as the days went by reaction came, and Crusoe gave way to morbid reflections. The dreariness of solitude gripped him for a time in brooding and despair, but what we may lay to a mixture of British phlegm—from Yorkshire, with a Teutonic leaven—came to his aid and saved his reason. There are consolations, he sees. He becomes a philosopher, and gives us the result of his cogitations. Crusoe does a vast amount of reflecting throughout the tale, but who would not? Twenty-eight years on a lonely island allow ample opportunity for reflection.

His first home is described in this wise:

Before I set up my tent, I drew a half-circle before the hollow place, which took in about ten yards in its semi-diameter from the rock, and twenty yards in its diameter. In this half-circle I pitched two rows of strong stakes, driving them into the ground till they stood very firm like piles, the biggest end being out of the ground about five foot and a half, and sharpened on the top. The two rows did not stand above six inches from one another. Then I took the pieces of cable which I cut in the ship, and laid them in rows one upon another, within the circle, between these two rows of stakes, up to the top, placing other stakes inside leaning against them, about two foot and a half high like a spur to a post; and this fence was so strong, that neither man nor beast could get into it, or over it. This cost me a great deal of time and labour, especially to cut the piles in the woods, bring them to the place, and drive them into the earth. The entrance into this place I made to be, not by a door, but by a short ladder, to go over the top; which ladder, when I was in, I lifted over after me, and so I was completely fenced in, and fortified, as I thought, from all the world, and consequently slept secure in the night, which otherwise I could not have done; though, as it appeared afterwards, there was no need of all this caution from the enemies that I apprehended danger from.

Having erected these defences and brought ashore the more pressing necessities of life, he found time for dangerous melancholia, and would fall into weeping at the realization of his dreadful plight. He believed that, since the island was uncharted and lying many leagues out in the Atlantic in waters unfrequented by shipping, he was doomed to end his wretched life there. Misery was his constant companion, until a naturally philosophical nature slowly began to drive out the black megrims of despair. I remember once reading the diary of a sheep-herder in Montana, who, after two months alone with nothing but the sheep to talk to, realized that he was slowly going mad. After the first week he ceased to shave—what was the need, with none but the stupid sheep to see him? Later he began to be careless about his clothes and the care of his cabin. He ceased to wash himself every day, began eating his food out of the cooking-pots. It was a dreadful picture of human degradation.

Before the end of the two months he had become a dirty, unshaven creature, going about talking aloud to himself, sinking lower than the animals he was supposed to attend to. Ponder upon this and be patient with Crusoe's despair. It was to his eternal credit (or Alexander Selkirk's, if you will) that he lived down these terrible moods.

And now being to enter into a melancholy relation of a scene of silent life, such, perhaps, as was never heard of in the world before,

I shall take it from its beginning, and continue it in its order. It was, by my account, the 30th of September when, in the manner as above said, I first set foot upon this horrid island, when the sun being in its autumnal equinox, was almost just over my head; for I reckoned myself by observation to be in the latitude of 9 degrees 22 minutes north of the line.

We can forgive Defoe for keeping secret the longitude. That would hardly do.

When reason, as Crusoe said, began to master his despondency he began to find what comfort he could get by setting the good against the evil in two columns, like debtor and creditor.

EVIL	GOOD
I am cast upon a horrible desolate island, void of all hope of recovery.	But I am alive, and not drowned, as all my ship's company was.
I am singled out and separated, as it were, from all the world, to be miserable.	But I am singled out too, from all the ship's crew to be spared from death; and He that miraculously saved me from death, can deliver me from this condition.
I am divided from mankind, a *solitaire*, one banished from human society.	But I am not starved and perishing on a barren place, affording no sustenance.
I have not cloathes to cover me.	But I am in a hot climate, where, if I had cloathes I could hardly wear them.
I am without any defence or means to resist any violence of man or beast.	But I am cast on an island, where I see no wild beasts to hurt me, as I saw on the coast of Africa; and what if I had been shipwrecked there?
I have no soul to speak to, or relieve me.	But God wonderfully sent the ship in near enough to the shore, that I have gotten out so many necessary things as will either supply my wants, or enable me to supply myself even as long as I live.

What a commentary on the instinct to live! Between a painless death and a painful life we choose the latter. I avow, meaning it, that I'd rather die than lose my eyes, but give me the choice and I should doubtless choose a sightless life to a painless oblivion. And so Crusoe. With all his repinings, he saw himself more fortunate than his late shipmates—now in Davy Jones's locker. Suicide may be said to be cowardice, but have we not a secret awe of those people who by suicide show such magnificent indifference to all that we ants struggle for? But then, if Crusoe had demonstrated his contempt for the undignified spectacle of men fighting against great odds to live, by himself jumping back into the sea that had spewed him up, we would have had no story and literature would have been considerably poorer in consequence.

When he had been on the island nearly a year he fell dangerously ill with some kind of fever, and in his journal relates a dream he had while in a delirium. This mad vision, which takes the form of an indescribably horrific creature sent to terrify Crusoe for neglecting his orisons, furnished Defoe with the opportunity and excuse for interpolating on Crusoe's behalf many passages and avowals of contrition for his godlessness. He remembers his father's advice and warning, when he had begged to be allowed to go to sea, that God would not prosper his adventures. From now on —*i.e.*, after the dream and his recovery—he applied himself to reading the Scriptures. Thereafter he daily read the Bible, of which three had been saved from the wreck. Having, in my own youth, set myself a similar task (but with less exalted purpose), namely, to read the Old and New Testaments through from beginning to end, I can commend the practice, if only because of the magnificent English to be found therein. The vow was accomplished, if I remember rightly, in something under three years.

In August, eleven months after being cast ashore, he makes the first mention of being happy. He speaks of beginning to enjoy himself. He had explored the island, and found it free from wild animals.

The introduction of the goats on the island in the story is suggestively one of the Alexander Selkirk touches, for on Juan Fernandez we know there were large herds of these ruminants. The grain he had sown was coming to fruition; there were grapes in abundance, and no stint of the meat of turtle, wild goats, and pigeons. About this time he caught the parrot which, after years of dumb companionship, was trained to speak. He now possessed a family of cats, a dog, a goat, and the parrot, the feline company having been augmented by a litter of kittens born on the island.

Here, in his journal, Crusoe makes a confession that is not without its humour. Referring to the improvement in his condition and its consequent effect on his outlook, he wrote:

> From this moment I began to conclude in my mind that it was possible for me to be more happy in this forsaken, solitary condition, than it was probable I should ever have been in any other particular state in the world; and with this thought I was going to give thanks to God for bringing me to this place. I know not what it was, but something shocked my mind at the thought, and I durst not speak the words. "How canst thou be such a hypocrite," said I, even audibly, "to pretend to be thankful for a condition which, however thou mayst endeavour to be contented with, thou wouldst pray heartily to be delivered from?"

It seems there is nothing like a desert island for teaching men philosophy. Hear Crusoe again. He had more than enough food—of a kind. He was his own master; he had health.

> I had no room for desire except it was of things which I had not, and they were but trifles, though indeed of great use to me. I had, as I hinted before, a parcel of money, as well gold as silver, about thirty-six pounds sterling. Alas! there the nasty, sorry, useless stuff lay; I had no manner of business for it; and I often thought with myself that I would have given a handful of it for a gross of tobacco pipes, or for a hand-mill to grind my corn; nay, I would have given it all for six-pennyworth of turnip and carrot seed out of England, or for a handful of peas and beans, and a bottle of ink.

The supply of ink from the ship's cabin had been eked out by dilution with water until it had become so pale that it scarcely showed its colour on paper. It was while writing in his journal one day with this watered ink that he remembered a strange concurrence of the dates of the major experiences of his life. On the 1st of September he had run away from home to go to sea. It was likewise on the 1st of September that he was captured by the Salee rover. He had also escaped from an earlier shipwreck and again from the Moors on this magic 1st of September.

About the fourth year of his exile his clothes, of which a goodly stock had been salved, now began to wear out. Forced by this circumstance to make shift with some other style of covering for his body—more against the power of the tropical sun and rain than from mere considerations of nakedness—he contrived the skin cap and clothing that are inseparable from a true visualization of Crusoe. Nor must we forget the umbrella by which our hero anticipated Jonas Hanway by a century.[1] This and the cap were most effective to " shoot off the rain." The skin hat was a high conical affair of goatskin, with a flap behind, both to keep off the rain and protect his neck from the sun. The breeches, reaching below the knee, were made of an old he-goat's skin. The jacket was also made of the same material. From the belt round his waist hung a small saw and a hatchet, and from a bandolier over his shoulder were suspended two skin bags, one for powder, the other for shot. Stockings and shoes he had none, but wore instead a skin wrapped round each leg and over his feet.

He had frequently pondered over the idea of putting to sea in a boat, but, after the abortive attempt to launch the ship's boat, which lay high and dry on the beach, and the failure to get a heavy canoe, fashioned after months of labour, into the water, he did not again attempt a maritime adventure until the fifth year, when he succeeded in hewing out and launching a small canoe, in which he ventured to cruise round his domain. He frequently asserts that he is a poor carpenter, poor tailor, in fact, a very incapable craftsman who made a botch of everything attempted, but, with time on his side, he seems to have turned out some very creditable makeshifts, all of which are carefully described.

[1] Jonas Hanway, who died in 1786, is said to have been the first Englishman to carry an umbrella, though umbrellas were known at a much earlier date.

Now comes the masterly description of the discovery of the footprint. The whole episode is pictured with remarkable fidelity to life; Crusoe's reactions to the discovery would be anyone's reactions in a similar circumstance. It is too long to quote—the matter occupies several pages of small type. The dreaded Caribs, a ferocious cannibal race, were known to inhabit the mainland. Instantly his thoughts flew to the Caribs. They had visited this sylvan paradise—might be at that moment watching him unseen. There was little sleep for Crusoe that night, nor the next, nor for three days, during which time he lay within his palisade watching for an enemy which did not come. And when eventually he went back and measured the footprint in vain hopes that it might after all be one of his own the discovery that the impression was much larger than his own further increased his sense of insecurity. This episode is undoubtedly one of the best and most convincing pieces of descriptive narrative in the entire book. I am sure that while writing it Defoe must have gone through all the torments suffered by his hero. He saw it too clearly not to have felt it. As for Crusoe, the discovery of the footprint had been such a shock that for the next years he lived in a state of constant apprehension.

THE FOOTPRINT

Then came the second shocking discovery—no less than

the finding of the bones of dead men near the cold ashes of a fire. This evidence of a cannibal feast so affected him that he was promptly sick, and left the scene more depressed than ever. He had been alone for fifteen years, and the first fine edge of his loneliness had left him. He wanted no visitors unless they were honest men, and now—the irony of it!— that his first visitors should be less welcome than would be wild beasts. But there was nothing he could do about it save further to fortify the defences begun after the discovery of the footprint two years previously.

Henceforth the tale moves faster, though actually some years have gone by. Crusoe is now in the twenty-third year of his exile. Twenty-three years alone! It defies imagination.

From the top of a hill he sees his first visitors, a group of nine naked savages squatting round a fire on the beach, where two canoes were drawn up. After they had gone Crusoe's indigna-

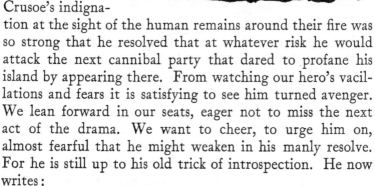

tion at the sight of the human remains around their fire was so strong that he resolved that at whatever risk he would attack the next cannibal party that dared to profane his island by appearing there. From watching our hero's vacillations and fears it is satisfying to see him turned avenger. We lean forward in our seats, eager not to miss the next act of the drama. We want to cheer, to urge him on, almost fearful that he might weaken in his manly resolve. For he is still up to his old trick of introspection. He now writes:

During all this time I was in a murdering humour, and took up most of my hours, which should have been better employed, in contriving how to circumvent and fall upon them the next time I should see them; especially if they should be divided, as they were the last time, into two parties. Nor did I consider at all that if I killed one party suppose ten or a dozen, I was still the next day, or week, or month, to kill another, and so another, even *ad infinitum*, till I should be at length no less a murderer than they were in being man-eaters, and perhaps much more so.

But our fears are needless. In good time Crusoe carries out his mighty vow of vengeance. Meanwhile there is another interval of a year or so, during which time he dreams one night that he attacks the savages and rescues a native, who becomes his devoted slave. This is only one of the many instances of Defoe's dabbling in the occult. As the months went by since the last visit of the cannibals Crusoe's impatience to be "up and at them" increased, until he began to scout for the foe. At last the day arrived, and the rescue of the wretched prisoner who became Friday. He is a

comely, handsome fellow, perfectly well made, with straight strong limbs, not too large, tall and well shaped, and as I reckon, about twenty-six years of age. . . . His hair was long and black, not curled like wool; his forehead very high and large, and a great vivacity and sparkling sharpness in his eyes.

The education of Friday proceeds apace, aided by the fellow's gratitude and a natural eagerness to make himself understood by his saviour. Alas! Friday is himself of the cannibal persuasion, and Crusoe is greatly shocked at his dusky companion's suggestion that they should eat the dead victims of the fight. However, he is subsequently educated to see the error of his ways.

With the coming of a companion Crusoe's life loses some of its unique attractiveness. Nor does the arrival of the Spaniards and Crusoe's rescue (accompanied by the faithful

Friday) in an English ship hold our attention as did those
first score of lonely years. He departed from the island
on December 19 in the year 1686, which was twenty-
eight years, two months, and nineteen days since he had
been cast ashore there. Defoe's passion for dates serves him
to the end.

It is quite surprising what a number of desert isle narratives of the Crusoe variety come to light after a little
searching. There is, for instance, the tale of the adventures
of Peter Wilkins, which seems to be a strange mixture of
Crusoe and Gulliver. The book appeared in London in
1751 under the title *The Life and Singular Adventures of
Peter Wilkins among the Flying Nations of the South Seas*, by
R. S. (The anonymous author was one Robert Paltock, an
attorney.) The story is fantastic and weird. Peter Wilkins
is the sole survivor of a shipwreck on a rocky, uncharted
coast. The ship is driven by the vast combers into a rocky
cavern, which turns out to be a tunnel leading into a
" prodigious lake of water." In the middle of this enormous
lake is an island, which becomes the home of Peter Wilkins.
It is an island within an island. He retrieves certain necessities from the wreck and builds himself an earthen house.
One day, while inside his dwelling, he hears a woman's
scream and a rustle of wings followed by a thud on the roof.
Running out, he finds a winged woman has descended from
the skies—an amiable, loving creature of gentle disposition,
whom he marries. Her name is a singularly ugly one—
Youwarkee—as are the names of the other winged people
he meets in this strange land. There is Mouch, Yacom, and
Glumm, names strongly reminiscent of Gulliver's friends.
The amiable Youwarkee presented Peter with numerous
progeny, and for many years they live in blissful seclusion.
But when, finally, her relations come across the water to live
with them Peter begins to lose interest in life. Their solitude is gone, and with it goes the spirit of Peter. So the tale

ends. This curious work was at one time sufficiently popular to justify its being frequently staged as a pantomime. I believe its last appearance was at the old Sadler's Wells Theatre.

Another Crusoe-inspired narrative, published in the same year as the Peter Wilkins book, was the history of one John Daniel, under the title of *A Narrative of the Life and Adventures of John Daniel*, by Ralph Morris, an unknown writer, or possibly a *nom de plume*. At any rate, he has never been identified. John Daniel began his adventures by doing a very unoriginal thing—he ran away from home and went to sea. He and a young shipmate called Thomas were the only survivors when their ship was wrecked on a desert island. The isle is described as sixty miles in circumference, heavily wooded, and populated with swine and wild cattle. They name the place appropriately Isle of Providence. The wreck conveniently proves an almost inexhaustible source of stores, which is fortunate, since the pair are destined to spend many years on this island. But that is not all. The story holds a delicious surprise for the reader.

One day Thomas is injured in a fall, and when John attends to his hurts he makes the astonishing discovery that his shipmate is really a woman. Now he recollects how he had frequently noticed in 'Thomas' certain gentle, feminine traits. Of course they marry, and, to do the thing *comme il faut*, a ring (made of catgut) is used, and they have a banquet of water and beef—all they have. In the course of time children are born, and as they reach maturity marry each other (a shocking irregularity here), and many take up homesteads of their own. One of the sons, a brainy lad called Jacob, builds out of material gathered from the wreck—chiefly "cotton and iron"—a flying machine. One day when father and son are pottering about with this machine, trying it out, they find themselves, willy-nilly, on the way to the moon. Arriving there, they meet with the most fantastic adventures and creatures half fish, half human. They

32

perform quite nonchalantly incredible feats, and equally incredibly return safely to their own Isle of Providence, where the now aged wife is at home grieving their absence. Other flying adventures follow, but John lives too long. Like the *struldbrugs* in Gulliver's island, he has become a little dull, and we are no longer interested in him. He dies unregretted at the age of ninety-five.

A castaway tale which appeared before Robinson Crusoe was Henry Neville's curious story *The Isle of Pines*, published in 1668. In the year 1589 a trading vessel named *India Merchant*, on a voyage to the Indies, is lost upon a reef off an unknown island somewhere off the coast of the Great South Land, or *Terra Australis Incognita*. Most of the company are lost, but there are five survivors, George Pine and four women! These, in order of rank, are the captain's daughter Sarah, two serving-maids, and a negress named Philippa. They are all youthful, and to avoid jealousies George decides to marry the lot. So this little Mormon community begins. They are quite happy, and Sarah presents her lord with fifteen children. Not to be outdone, the two maids become in the course of time mothers of thirty children between them: one seventeen, the other thirteen. Then there is the dusky Philippa, who bears him twelve piccaninnies. Many years later a Dutch ship, having been blown far out of her course, comes upon this island, and sends a boat ashore. The Dutchmen find it governed by William Pine, grandson to the original George and head of no less than 1789 of his descendants. Those who distrust Henry Neville's multiplication may work it out for themselves.

Shakespeare's mysterious enchanted island in *The Tempest* has always had a romantic fascination for me. It is known, of course, that the poet partly identified it with the then little-known island of Bermuda, which Jourdain called " The Isle of Devils," slandering that fair country so outrageously that when Sir George Somers was wrecked there he was agreeably surprised to find that the island had been so unfairly defamed. But the slander served a purpose by giving Shakespeare the eerie background he desired for *The Tempest* plot, and so we should be grateful. Bermuda can afford to ignore the slander. What a place it was, its dark woods populated with spirits, fairies, witches. Among them is the ungainly Caliban, swinging ape-like through the undergrowth, and the lightsome Ariel, dancing like a moonbeam in the surrounding gloom. And within his cell sits the embittered Prospero, weaving his spells and commanding the unseen creatures of the dark forest. Somewhere in the background, for we never see her, is the evil Sycorax, the witch, and the antithesis of the sweet Miranda, who until the shipwreck had never seen the features of any man save Prospero, her father. Was there ever such a fortunate shipwreck? A maid and a man (Ferdinand) united in an idyllic love, a wrong righted, and finally the departure from the island, with Prospero's necromantic books buried deep in the earth, and the release from the trees of the prisoners of the sorceress Sycorax. Nevertheless, one somehow regrets the departure of the company from this sombrely fascinating, enchanted isle.

CALIBAN

The only isles in English fiction to compare with it are those fantastic islands stumbled upon by Lemuel Gulliver, Esquire; to wit, Lilliput, Brobdingnag, the land of the

34

Houyhnhnms, and the Island of Laputa, where the half-mad people employed professional 'flappers,' who would from time to time rouse their masters from a sort of day-dreaming by gently flicking their mouths or ears with bladders. Nothing, indeed, could be more fantastic than Gulliver's experiences in the group of islands best known under the comprehensive title of Laputa. Here in the country of the Balnibarbi he met the unfortunate *struld-brugs*, human beings doomed to live for ever, and marked out from their more fortunate fellow-creatures by the ominous birth-spot on their foreheads. Laputa, the island of theorists, of clumsy, maladroit people, obsessed with theories and crazy dreams of how life should be lived, is Swift's best satire, better even than the portrait of men as Yahoos, the disgusting beasts in the land of the gentle Houyhnhnms. And the curious nomenclature of Gulliver! In Lilliput some of the more important people bear such fantastic names as Clesren, Frelock, Flimnap, and Golbasto, the six-inch-high Emperor; while in Brobdingnag the little nurse—a mere forty feet in height, and small for her age— rejoices in the name of Glumdalclitch. Gulliver, who was taken to the metropolis, Lorbrulgrud, to be shown to the king, was named by her Grildrig, meaning mannikin. But I must desist—this is hardly Crusoe matter.

Getting back to Crusoe's acknowledged followers, the most notorious of these is *The Swiss Family Robinson*,[1] the creation of Johann David Wyss, a book which so upset Captain Marryat that he wrote *Masterman Ready* as a sort of protest—to produce something more accurate and less offensive to common intelligence than the history of Robin-son Crusoe's Swiss namesakes. The only excuse we have for this preposterous volume is that it was written for children. That ponderous-minded family, so related in sentiment to the Fairchild Family, and so providentially spared out of all the crew of their wrecked ship during a voyage to Otaheiti,

---

[1] *Schweizerischer Robinson.*

where Papa Robinson was to take up a post as minister, find themselves on a perfect island. The thing was too easy; everywhere they found what they needed, and the wreck was an inexhaustible storehouse of everything needful for their comforts ashore. The sentiment is mawkish and false, the topography, the fauna, and the flora unrelated to each

SWISS FAMILY ROBINSON
adapted from an old print

other. For example, on this tropical island are kangaroos, buffaloes, agoutis, eagles, wild asses, tortoises, ostriches, boa-constrictors, crocodiles and alligators, sea-cows, and wolves!

But Fritz, Jack, Ernest, and little Francis found it all delightful (as indeed it must have been), and had such a grand time that ten years later, when they were rescued by a passing ship, only two of the family, the eldest and the youngest, were willing to leave. Jack and Ernest, now young men of twenty and twenty-two, preferred remaining behind with their ageing parents (parents aged earlier those days), who wisely chose to end their days on their island rather than venture after so long an absence once more into the hurly-burly of civilization. It is tempting to scoff at their ridiculous smugness, and the dreary dissertations of *pater familias* upon the various natural phenomena, but it

THE SWISS FAMILY ROBINSON EDEN

would be churlish not to notice the friendly sentiments of the author for the British flag. For it was an English ship— the *Unicorn*—that found them.

So Fritz and Francis return in the *Unicorn* to Europe, and it is from Fritz that we get the story of the Swiss Family Robinson. The old father wrote to his sons on departure:

I finish these last few lines whilst the ship's boat is waiting. My sons will thus receive my last blessing. May God ever be with

37

you! Adieu, Europe! Adieu, dear Switzerland! Never shall I see you again! May your inhabitants be always happy, pious, and free!

Here we will leave the Crusoes of fiction for the Crusoes of fact, aware that we have by no means exhausted the list of classic castaways.

CHAPTER II

The Lonely Exile of Alexander Selkirk

I am Monarch of all I survey;
    My right there is none to dispute;
From the centre all round to the sea
    I am lord of the fowl and the brute.
O Solitude! where are the charms
    That sages have seen in thy face?
Better dwell in the midst of alarms,
    Than reign in this horrible place.

. . . . .

But the sea-fowl is gone to her nest;
    The beast is laid down in his lair;
Even here is a season of rest,
    And I to my cabin repair.
There's mercy in every place,
    And mercy, encouraging thought!
Gives even affliction a grace
    And reconciles man to his lot.

W. COWPER

THE first accurate account of Selkirk's life on Juan
Fernandez appeared in Captain Woodes Rogers'
narrative of his privateering cruise to the South Seas.
This book was published in 1712—*i.e.*, seven years before
Robinson Crusoe—but, curiously enough, no one was heard
to accuse Daniel Defoe of using Selkirk's narrative, though
many of his readers charged him with foisting a fantastic and incredible story on to the public. Defoe took the

outcry much to heart, and, as other artists have done when challenged by the unimaginative Doctor Dryasdusts, endeavoured—not very successfully—to explain himself to their satisfaction, which, of course, was a mistake. The justification, or explanation, took the form of a declaration in the preface to the *Serious Reflections of Robinson Crusoe*, and purported to be signed by Crusoe himself.

> I, Robinson Crusoe, being at this time in perfect and sound memory (thanks be to God therefor), do hereby declare, their objection is an invention, scandalous in design, and false in fact; and do affirm, that the story, though allegorical, is also historical; and that it is the beautiful representation of a life of unexampled misfortunes; and of a variety not to be met with in the world: sincerely adapted to, and intended for the common good of mankind; and designed at first, as it is now further applied, to the most serious uses possible.

Whether believed or not, it became instantly a bestseller, edition after edition being quickly sold out. On the Continent it was translated and widely pirated. The newfound art of realistic narrative had captured the public fancy, and had come to stay. In his preface to *Naufragia*[1] James Stanier Clarke, touching on the twin subjects Robinson Crusoe and Alexander Selkirk, wrote:

> Before we enter on the more solemn and awful subjects of this little Volume, it appeared to me not irrelevant to pay some attention to the character, which, whether known under the real name of Alexander Selkirk or the fictitious one of Robinson Crusoe, has always been considered, if I may so express myself, as the venerable recorder of the shipwrecked Narrative. When I recollect the avidity with which the page of *Crusoe* has been perused from its appearance in 1719, the wide circulation it obtained on the Continent, and the peculiar delight it afforded me when a schoolboy; it seems astonishing, rather that a work of this kind should not have been previously undertaken, than that it should now be offered to the attention of the public. *Robinson Crusoe* does not

---

[1] In two volumes, London, 1805.

yield even to *Gil Blas* in the universal suffrage it has experienced; and yet the supposed authors of each seem to be equally surreptitious and doubtful. Though they are both read and admired; a specious Frenchman, who never composed a single original work of merit, enjoys the reputation of the one, whilst Alexander Selkirk and Defoe, with more reason, divide the credit of the other.

As most people know, Alexander Selkirk, or Selcraig, the prototype of Robinson Crusoe and the inspiration for Cowper's poem, passed his Crusoe-like exile on the island, or one of the islands, of Juan Fernandez, which lies in the Pacific some 400 miles from Valparaiso. Juan Fernandez is really a scattered group of three islands, two large and one small. The island immortalized by Selkirk is known as Más-a-Tierra, and is twelve and a half miles long by three and two-thirds miles at its widest part. A mile to the south-west lies the islet of Santa Clara, sometimes called Goat Island. Literally translated, the name Más-a-Tierra means "nearer in"—*i.e.*, nearer to the mainland than the second of the larger two islands, which lies a hundred miles farther west, and is known as Más-a-Fuera, which is to say, "farther to sea." The latter is considerably smaller than Más-a-Tierra. The group was first sighted in 1563 by a Spanish navigator, Juan Fernández, after whom it was named. Its history is closely woven with the privateers and buccaneers who used it, especially Más-a-Tierra, as a watering-place and rendezvous for over two hundred years. Fernández obtained from Spain a grant of the islands, and himself took possession by settling there for a time. It was the goats and pigs he left there which, by multiplying in such great numbers, provided fresh meat for the freebooters who came that way later. In 1616, many years after Fernández had departed, two navigators, Willem Cornelis Schouten and Jacob le Maire, called to replenish their water-casks, and found the hills overrun with the semi-wild descendants of the Fernández livestock.

A Spanish memorial, published in 1773 by a Mr Dalrymple, tells how Fernández came upon the islands by accident while making from one port to another on the west coast of South America. Fernández had found out that in order to reach ports lying to the south he could gain them more easily by standing out to sea and then sailing 'diagonally' in than he could have done by inshore navigation. Thus, taking a long reach out to sea to avoid the contrary winds met on the coast, he came by accident upon Más-a-Tierra. Till 1749 the islands remained anybody's property, but at that date the Spanish Government, hearing that Anson was in favour of British occupation, sent a garrison there, and in the following year formally annexed them in the name of the King of Spain. They remained Spanish territory until Chile won her independence early in the nineteenth century, when she took them over. Until 1840 they were used principally as a penal settlement, the convicts being housed in caves. But Chile's hold seems to have been at first very lax, for in 1835 an Englishman named Sutcliffe set up as the self-styled Governor. Apparently it was not worth while interfering with him. Then in 1867 a shipchandler named Flint leased the main island, Más-a-Tierra, from the Chilians, but failed to make the venture pay. In the following year Commodore Powell, of H.M.S. *Topaze*, landed, and had a tablet erected to the memory of Alexander Selkirk on the eminence known as Selkirk's Look-out. On the tablet was inscribed the date of his coming ashore from the galley *Cinque Ports*, 1704, and the time of his departure, February 12, 1709. Since then it has been frequently visited by noted travellers. Captain Joshua Slocum, who won fame by his lone voyage around the world in the middle nineties, called there in the spring of 1896, and immediately fell in love with the place. With Yankee enterprise he sold the islanders several hundredweight of tallow which he had salved from a wreck off Tierra del Fuego. It is of more interest to hear that he was paid in curious old coins, some of which had been brought up from the wreck of a galleon sunk in Cumberland Bay, the only anchorage close inshore. Slocum, described it as the "blessed island," and confessed that he wondered how Robinson Crusoe could have borne to leave such a delightful spot.

In spite of this the isle was more than once abandoned by hopefuls who had tried to settle there. Calling ships would bring back reports of the wretched condition of the exiles. In the year 1890 the population, which had dwindled to sixty people, lived in hovels and eked out a miserable livelihood trading seal, goat-skins, and fish for flour and other stores brought by ships. All this is very conflicting, and the only way to find out whether Captain Slocum was right is to make a personal call and see for oneself. Captain Vancouver, calling at Juan Fernandez on his way home from his Pacific cruise in 1795, described the island as not being very attractive from the sea.

> The whole composed a group of broken irregular hills, forming altogether as rude and grotesque a Scene as the imagination can well fancy.

Another writer describes it (I refer always to Más-a-Tierra) as beautiful, and speaks of its consisting

> of a series of precipitous volcanic rocks which are rudely piled into irregular blocks and pinnacles, and strongly contrasting with a rich vegetation.

The loftiest of the pinnacles is a rock known as El Yunque, "The Anvil," 3225 feet. The fauna and flora is more or less the same as that of Chile. The original forests, mainly sandalwood, have almost disappeared through the short-sighted greed of past generations of colonists, who reaped without afterward sowing. There were no indigenous mammals. The cattle, horses, goats, swine, and dogs now so common were, with the exception of the latter two animals, unknown there in Selkirk's day.

Incidentally, the famous Scotsman was not the first man to be marooned on Más-a-Tierra. In 1680 a certain Captain Bartholomew Sharpe, cruising in those waters, sighted the island, and, standing down to it, sent a party ashore. Finding the country uninhabited, he christened it Queen Katharine Island. Shortly afterward the crew mutinied, deposed Sharpe, and elected a certain Watling as captain. While this was going on three Spanish sail were

sighted, and the Englishmen stood not upon the manner of their going, but up-anchored and fled to sea with more haste than dignity. Some of the crew were ashore when the signal came to return in all haste to the ship. All got off but one —a poor Mosquito Indian who had gone into the woods after wild goats. Here he was marooned, and lived entirely alone, until three years later he was rescued by Dampier's ship in March 1684. Now Dampier, who had spent the early part of his life in shady company, had been a member of the crew on Watling's vessel when it had suddenly to put to sea to escape the Dons. But he had not forgotten the Indian, and on his second round-the-world voyage called at

44

Juan Fernandez [1] (March 22, 1684) to see if the unfortunate native was still there. Dampier describes the meeting. The first man ashore was a fellow-Indian named Robin, who, running up the beach, quickly showed the timid castaway that he was amongst friends. He was dressed in goat-skins and carried a spear, the head of which he had hammered out of his gun-barrel. Captain Cowley, of Dampier's ship, describes the meeting:

> Now the Man, when he saw our Ships, presently fancied us to be English, and thereupon went and catched three goats, and dressed them against our men came on shoar; there being several of our ship's company who were at the leaving of the Indian there by Captain Sharpe, and among others Captain Edward Cooke and Mr William Dampier.

During the Indian's exile he had several times been hunted by calling Spaniards, who had either seen him from the sea or discovered his hut when they came ashore. He preferred his terrible isolation to the dangerous company of the Spaniards, who were not famed for their humanity to the Indians. When he had been left behind all he possessed was a musket, a knife, a horn of powder, and a handful of shot. But, with an Indian's sagacity, he at once began making the most of what he had, and built himself a small hut half a mile back from the sea, lining it with goat-skins. His couch, called a barbecue, was raised on short sticks two feet off the ground. At first his only food was the meat of seal, but later when he began to kill the wild goats he used only the seal's skin, with which he made thongs. These thongs served for fish-line, for rope, for thread and string, and for binding wood in place of nails. He saw Dampier's ship the day before it had come in to anchor, and had recognized her as an English craft by the cut of her jib. Feeling that he was going to be rescued at last, he prepared a feast for his friends by killing three goats. When Robin, the other

----

[1] He spelled it John Fernando.

Mosquito Indian, went up to him he fell flat on his face by way of greeting. The other lifted him up, and the pair reversed the process, doubtless an old Indian custom. The unimaginative sailors had dubbed the marooned aboriginal Will—not even William. But it was said that he was proud of his simple cognomen, for the tribe were so poor and wretched that among themselves they had no names, a statement that one is loath to believe.

Quite a number of former-day navigators, buccaneers, and privateers have described Juan Fernandez. Ringrose, Dampier, Clarke, Woodes Rogers, Shelvocke, Anson, and Cooke—not Cook—have all given us their impressions. Captain Edward Cooke, after his voyage round the world (1708–11), wrote, "Here are two islands together, the biggest whereof is three leagues and one half in length." On approach it seemed to be nothing but rocks without vegetation, the tops of which were hidden in low-hanging clouds. He speaks of anchoring in a stately bay (Cumberland Bay) and of seeing herds of goats. Cooke was himself compelled to spend two nights ashore through the ship's being forced to run to sea, and he complains that the noise of the seals on the beach spoiled his sleep, and drove him into the hills in order to get some rest. On the third day the ship returned, and took on board the captain,who was glad to leave the place. But every one was grateful for the two hundred jars of fresh water they had secured from the island's streams.

Commodore George Anson, during his historic voyage round the world (1740–4) in the *Centurion*, was glad to put into Cumberland Bay for a rest and refit after one of the most heartbreaking passages on record. Not only had he nearly lost his ship in a succession of terrible gales, but his men were dying at the rate of six a day. Labouring up the west coast, half a wreck, with jury [1] rigging, her spars cracked, and her hull leaking like a basket, the *Centurion*, seeking the rendezvous of Juan Fernandez, actually missed

---

[1] Jury—*i.e.*, makeshift.

the island, and nearly two weeks were spent searching for it. By this unfortunate delay another sixty men died who might have been saved had they been put ashore a fortnight sooner. The *Centurion* anchored in the bay with only two hundred out of her original five hundred men alive. To Anson the island looked forbidding, but none the less welcome. Closer inshore he remarked the deep, shaded valleys, the heavily wooded hills, and in one place a waterfall a hundred feet high dropping down a sheer cliff.

The story of Alexander Selkirk is inseparable from that of Captains Dampier, Woodes Rogers, and Stradling.

Twenty-five years after Indian Will had been picked up by Dampier and Captain Cowley, to be exact, on January 31, 1709, Dampier, who was again in these waters (the man's affection for the sea was incurable), was witness to a rescue more momentous than that of the poor Indian. Captain Woodes Rogers, in the privateer *Duke*, of which Dampier was sailing master,[1] sighted Juan Fernandez, where he had come to take on fresh water. As they approached the land after nightfall they were astonished to see lights on the shore, and were by no means easy in their minds about it, half fearing that the lights indicated the presence of a French squadron. Standing well off during the night, they were relieved to find by daylight no ships at anchor or at sea. The lights they had mistaken for a possible enemy were the fires of our hero, Alexander Selkirk, who, as a boat was sent ashore, was seen — a wild, skin-clad figure — running down the beach to meet it. After four years and four months bereft of the companionship of fellow-humans he had lost the power of fluent speech, and his greetings were hardly intelligible. "We could scarce understand him," wrote Woodes Rogers. On board the *Duke* he was offered rum, but refused it. It was a long time before he could relish the ship's unpalatable stores, and he was full of praise for the island fruits, especially a species of small black plum

[1] A position long since obsolete.

47

found on trees growing on the higher hills and rocks, and, like gold, difficult to come by.

Selkirk, the seventh son of a Largo[1] (Fifeshire) cobbler, had had a chequered career at sea, for he was a man of quick

temper and an adventurous spirit. His last berth, previous to his exile on Juan Fernandez, had been as sailing master in the galley *Cinque Ports*. Not being able to get along with the notorious Captain Stradling of that vessel, he requested to be put ashore on the island, a request almost immediately regretted when it was too late. He was landed with his

[1] There is a stone statue of him in the village now.

SELKIRK

sea-chest, bedding, spare clothes, a few religious books, knife-hatchet, mathematical instruments, a firelock, one pound of gunpowder, a bag of bullets, and a steel and flint.

The first eight months of solitude was the crucial period —after that he became more used to it. At first he contemplated suicide, roaming aimlessly about the island for weeks, practically bereft of sanity. At night he lay shivering in terror, but he was young —under thirty— and Nature presently began to adjust the balance, restoring somewhat his peace of mind, and in time pulling him entirely out of his Slough of Despond. He began to hunt and fish, catching turtles and goats, and building himself a second hut near by. The second and smaller hut he used for dressing his meat; the larger for sleeping. They were built with the trimmed trunks and branches of the pimento tree. These dwellings were not so elaborate as Crusoe's, but they kept out the wind and rain, which is the main thing for vulnerable man. Both were thatched with grass and had their interiors lined with dried goat-skins. Selkirk was known for an ingenious fellow on board ship (Dampier described him as the best man they had), but now he found himself hard put to it to provide such necessities that came so easily to the Indians. Learning to obtain fire by rubbing two sticks together took so long that he would frequently do without fire. His going ashore seems to have been carried out with injudicious haste, for he had brought no salt, and now, when everything had to be eaten saltless, he felt its absence keenly. There was no

corn for breadmaking, but he found a few turnips previously sown by Dampier, also the wild plum already mentioned, besides goat meat and crayfish gathered on the shore. He, too, noticed the barking of the seals (or sea-lions), which had kept Captain Cooke awake. These came ashore in the autumn "to whelp and engender." When his ammunition came to an end it did not much matter, for by that time he

was so strong and so used to the wild life that he could catch the goats by his fleetness of foot. Speaking of Selkirk's prowess as a runner, Woodes Rogers said:

> Indeed, he could run with wonderful swiftness through the woods, over rocks and up hills, as we found out when he caught goats for us. . . . We had a bull-dog which we sent along with him and with several of our swiftest runners, but Selkirk outstripped them all, both dog and men, captured the goats and brought them to us on his back.

During the years on the island Selkirk estimated that he had killed no less than five hundred goats. Once, when pursuing a goat to the edge of a cliff, he slipped, and fell to the bottom. Twenty-four hours later he regained consciousness, and found he was lying on the dead quarry, a position which had probably saved his life. Crawling to the hut a mile distant, he lay for ten days, too sore and ill to stir out. After a year or so he learned to like the saltless food, and thereafter did not miss the *sine qua non* of a civilized *cuisine*. Men are remarkably adaptable when they must be. The Canadian-Scandinavian explorer, Stefansson, who discovered the 'blond' Eskimos, lived as a native for months on a purely meat diet without salt —and liked it.

The crayfish were as large as lobsters and very succulent, but the lack of salt was a great hardship, and several attacks of dysentery Selkirk attributed to a saltless diet. He soon found that the fruit of the pimento made an excellent substitute for pepper, and thereafter used it. He also mentions, besides the turnips, 'cabbages' from the cabbage-tree.

A plague of rats was the cause of his breeding a family of cats as a means of self-protection, and these were his only domestic pets.[1] Robinson Crusoe, with his goat, dog, parrot, and cats fared better.

Apparently Selkirk's clothes wore out quicker than did Crusoe's, for ere long he was having to sew up goat-skins for body covering. His shoes, too, wore out, but the soles of his feet had grown as hard as an African's, and, in fact, after going on board the *Duke* it was a long time before he could endure to wear boots. His skin clothing, with the hair outward to shed the rain, was cleverly stitched with thongs, a nail being used to prick the holes in the tough

material. When, after serving its purpose of maid of all work, his knife wore down to the back he succeeded in making others out of hoop-iron picked up on the beach, beaten straight, and, with much labour, ground thin on stones. Lest a false impression is given by the statement about his skin clothing (and the pundits are without mercy to the erring historian), we are bound to confess that our hero wore a linen shirt beneath the skin coat. He had never been without that garment of civilization, though when found he was on his last shirt, as it were, for he had made it out of a strip of linen hoarded in his chest, the 'thread' for sewing coming from the worsted of an unravelled stocking.

What an existence, hunting, eating, and sleeping! But had he no diversions, no amusements whatever ? He had, but of a sort that would scarcely satisfy a less philosophical man. To the cats, which would "lie about in hundreds," he would sing and dance, so his historian wrote. He also

---

[1] The cats had come ashore from visiting ships, and were semi-wild.

53

tamed some of the kids to follow him about. Again he would find diversion in carving his own name on trees, with the dates. Crusoe set up a board with the date of his being washed ashore. Selkirk had his religious books, which he read with an enjoyment that might be difficult to understand in these hurried modern days. As an alternative to reading he would sing or pray—a great panacea for an undoubting castaway. He avowed afterward that during his

exile he became a better Christian than he had ever been before or ever had been since. Occasionally Spaniards invaded his solitude, attracted by his fires, and hunted the island for him. And he, in terror of being murdered or put to slavery in a Spanish mine, would flee to the hills and hide high in the top of a tall tree, until they gave up the search and departed. Once a group of pursuers searched the bushes at the foot of the very tree he was hiding in. The trees were the pimentos, some sixty feet high,[1] and cotton-trees, with boles of vast girth. There were no palms, as the island is within the temperate zone. The summer heat is

[1] My second authority puts thirty feet as their maximum height.

moderate, and during the winter months (our summer-time) there is sometimes a slight frost. It speaks for the temperateness of the climate that the verdure remains green all the year round.

The *Duke* remained two weeks at Juan Fernandez before continuing her amiable purpose of harassing Spanish shipping and raiding coastal towns. During the ship's stay there Selkirk did very valuable service in catching the wild goats whose meat greatly aided the recovery of many of the scurvy and other sick cases on board. Among the prizes taken was a vessel which Woodes Rogers refitted, re-christened the *Increase*, and put in charge of Selkirk as captain. And so from the peaceful life of lonely castaway he entered upon the busy and hazardous profession of privateer. He was taken off Juan Fernandez in February 1709, but did not reach England till October 1711. In the following year he returned to his native town of Largo, and took unto himself a wife, but five years later we again find him at sea. He died in 1721 while still in service. His last ship was H.M.S. *Weymouth*, on which he served in the capacity of master's mate. By his long exile on Juan Fernandez he had been spared what was perhaps a worse fate, for a few months after he had quitted the *Cinque Ports* she ran ashore in bad weather, and her crew were taken prisoners by the Spanish, who treated them with the utmost harshness.

When Selkirk's story became known he found himself moderately famous—to his great embarrassment. He was interviewed by Sir Richard Steele, who lost no time in spreading his fame abroad. At a house in Bristol, the home of Mrs Damaris Daniel, he met a man described as of medium height, somewhat thin, of dark features, grey eyes, hooked nose, a sharp chin, and brown hair covered by a wig. This unattractive picture purports to describe a man already well known in the literary world, one Daniel Defoe. Now there are many who have criticized this literary gentleman

55

in no uncertain terms for 'stealing' Selkirk's story. I do not propose to enter into the discussion. It is enough that he gave us Robinson Crusoe. Mavor, writing in 1797, says rather bitterly:

> . . . and it should be here remarked what indeed few are ignorant of—that when Selkirk came to England he was advised to put his papers into the hands of the celebrated Daniel Defoe to arrange for publication. But that ingenious literary pirate, converting the original material, by the aid of a luxurious fancy, into the well-known romance of *Robinson Crusoe*, thus defrauded Selkirk of the emolument which, it was reasonable to suppose, he might have reaped from his unaffected narrative of his solitary occupations and thoughts.

Perhaps so.

In the periodical *The Englishman* [1] Sir Richard Steele wrote of his meeting with Selkirk.

> When I first saw him I thought if I had not been let into his Character and Story, I could have discerned that he had been much separated from company, from his aspect and gesture. There was a strong but cheerful seriousness in his look, and a certain disregard to the ordinary things about him as if he had been sunk in thought. . . . The man frequently bewailed his return to the World, which could not, he said, with all its enjoyments, restore him to the tranquillity of his Solitude. Though I had frequently conversed with him, after a few months' absence he met me in the street, and though he spoke to me I could not recollect that I had seen him: familiar converse in this town had taken off the loneliness of his aspect, and quite altered his face.

He received £800 in prize money (a large sum in the eighteenth century) as his share in the Acupulco galleon taken by Woodes Rogers. After receiving the prize money he made the characteristic remark, "I am now worth eight hundred pounds; but I shall never be so happy as when I was not worth a farthing." This remark is quite consistent with his conduct after his return to Fifeshire, where for a

[1] December 3, 1713.

time he lived as a hermit in a cave dug in his own garden.
He would walk the hills alone, speaking to no one. His marriage was an elopement with a cowherdess named Sophia
Bruce, but does not seem to have been particularly successful, as he afterward left her.

Apart from Woodes Rogers' account of Selkirk's experience, there was his own story, entitled *Providence Displayed,
or a Surprising Account of one Alexander Selkirk* . . . (1712),
written by his own hand. His story also appeared in Captain Edward Cooke's *A Voyage to the South Sea and Round
the World* (1712), Funnell's *Voyage Round the World* (1707),
and *The Life and Adventures of Alexander Selkirk*, by John
Howell (1829).

CHAPTER III

The Misfortunes of Richard Falconer

Bold were the Men who on the Ocean first
Spread their New Sails, when Shipwreck was the worst.
More danger now from Man alone we find,
Than from the Rocks, the Billows, or the Wind.

WALLER

THIS doggerel appeared in the 1720 edition of *The Voyages, dangerous Adventures and imminent Escapes of Captain Richard Falconer*,[1] a work whose authenticity cannot be vouched for, but which, nevertheless, is too rare and diverting to be omitted on that score. The author, in an amusing preface which I will quote in full, in apologizing for his shortcomings as a literary person, says, "but Truth is amiable tho' in Rags." So let us take him at his word, and there's no harm done. His preface (in a day when prefaces, introductions, forewords, apologias, explanatory notes, dedications to noble patrons, proems, prologues, preambles, and such-like overtures were apt to be humourless and ponderous affairs) is, in its disarming candour, quite whimsical, as though he was writing with his tongue in his cheek.

I am told that a Book without a Preface is like a New Play without a prologue, or a French Dinner without Soup; and tho' I cannot tell what to say, yet I am resolved to say something, tho' perhaps not anything to the Purpose. So far I hope you'll allow

---

[1] This book is believed to have been printed prior to *Robinson Crusoe*.

me to be an Author. I shall give you, gentle Reader (if you are so), Three of my Reasons why I publish these following Pages; which, I must confess, are not so well polished as I cou'd wish, but Truth is amiable tho' in Rags. The first and chiefest, to get Money; for tho' I have a considerable Income, yet I can never bring both points together at the Years' End; but however don't blame my Oeconomy, since I owe you nothing, and if I am beholden to any Body it is my Bookseller; (I beg his Pardon if I miscall him, tho' I don't believe it will anger him in the least, for all men love to be termed so, whether they deserve it or no) being he will run the greatest Risque if my Book does not sell. Second, to save my Lungs, and a great deal of Trouble in repeating to my Friends these following Adventures, for now they may be at a small Expence to get 'em by Heart, if they will endeavour to stretch their Memories. Third and lastly to appear in Print, which was, I assure you a great Motive with me as well as with a great many others of the same Rank, that make Work for many Printers, tho' as little to the Purpose as myself. I cou'd give a Catalogue of some of 'em, but that would be making my Preface exceed the Bulk of my Book, tho' I cou'd put the Booksellers in a Way to save Money in their Pockets, and that is to persuade a great many Authors to print their Lucubrations at their own Charge, and that might make some of the poorest to desist; but for the richer sort of Authors, there's no Help, it's like the Itch, and they must write to be scratched until the Blood comes. The following Sheets, however extraordinary they appear, I assure you upon the Word of a Man are Truth, and I hope they will entertain you; but if they don't, and you should chance to slight 'em, you will not anger,

Your Servant,

CANTERBURY   R. FALCONER
November 7, 1719

In the fourth edition (1734) appears an additional preface —a preface to a preface.

'Tis in compliance with Sir Roger L'Estrange's maxim, "That a Man has as good go to Court without a Cravat as appear in Print without a Preface," that I give the gentle Reader any interruption of this kind: for to be plain with him, the Book itself, as full of Misfortunes as it is, is but a Preface to the Misfortunes I have met with since its first publication; which, I must freely confess, are wholly owing to the bent of my own headstrong inclination, in not taking my Father's advice, at my first setting out into the world. . . .

Richard Falconer[1] was born some time about 1680, at Bruton, in Somerset. His mother dying while he was a child, he was left in the care of his father, who was a tax official, and, as things went in the seventeenth century, he was tolerably well off. From some ancestor Falconer *cadet* had inherited an insatiable passion for the sea, but for a long time his father remained unmoved to all the boy's persuasions to be allowed to go to sea. However, the elder Falconer got into money difficulties, and saw that it would perhaps be more convenient if the boy was allowed his wish. So he was sent to Bristol with a letter to a certain Captain Pultney and £100 in the lining of his clothes. This money was to keep him in lodgings and to pay for his studies in mathematics and navigation. The time came when he was sent aboard the *Albion*, frigate, Captain Wase commanding. The frigate sailed for Jamaica on May 2, 1699, and after sundry adventures that have no bearing on our story arrived at Port Royal four months later. Here he pauses to describe the islands, their people, and the rough life there. The Gulf of Mexico and the Caribbean Sea were infested with pirates who terrorized both land and sea. The favourite *pied-à-terre* of the buccaneers was Tortuga (Turtle) Island, off the coast of Haiti, and no unprotected ship dare approach this island with impunity. The logwood cutters of Panama, Yucatan, Hispaniola, and Cuba were as rough a set of men as you could meet in a year's travel, and were but one stage removed from pirates. They and the wild-cattle hunters, who lived in crude huts called *boucans*— hence *boucanier*, or buccaneer in English—would steal and sell the logwood belonging to their employers, or capture some small, unsuspecting craft and go a-pirating. But there

[1] Not to be confused with William Falconer (1732-69), who wrote the long poem *The Shipwreck* and *Falconer's Marine Dictionary*.

was said to be money in the logwood trade if you could find some virgin spot, cut your own timber, and convey it by sea to the nearest market.

Falconer, a restless young man, became fired with a desire to adventure in this trade, and as the frigate would be at Port Royal for some months he appealed for and was granted leave to go with a number of shipmates in a sloop to Campeachy Bay for logwood—a perfectly honest expedition. The sloop was shortly afterward fitted out and stored with water and provisions for the passage, and left Port Royal for Campeachy. Cruising along the coast, stopping here and there, the adventurers bargained with the *boucaniers* for their wood, always, however, with their pistols within reach. But nothing untoward happened, and with her holds full of the heavy wood the sloop sailed for Jamaica.

The day which actually marks the beginning of Richard Falconer's misfortunes was a balmy one, so warm the air and calm the sea that Falconer lay idling in a boat towed astern, with a well-thumbed volume of Ovid for company. Lulled by soft airs into a state of drowsiness, he lay back with no

inkling of the disaster that came a few minutes later, when an unseen, unnoticed squall of wind and rain descended upon sloop and boat towing astern. Awakened rudely, Falconer, understanding the danger, hauled on the wet painter to bring himself close  aboard, so to regain the sloop by climbing over her stern. But the strain of the heavy boat broke the painter, and the boat quickly fell astern, bobbing and rolling so violently as to throw out her lone passenger. Hearing Falconer's shouts, and running aft to sense the cause, then seeing the boat adrift, his [companions hove the sloop to, and tried to run down to him to effect a

rescue. It had happened so swiftly that there was at first no realizing the seriousness of the accident. But after some time spent in searching for their hapless shipmate, now hopelessly lost behind a curtain of drifting mists and rain, they decided that he had been drowned, and so mournfully gave up the search, to resume once more the course for Jamaica.

Meanwhile Falconer, by no means drowned, is drifting at the whim of winds and sea, he knows not whither, for he has neither compass nor chart. For about four hours he swam, and drifted thus until at the coming of dusk he felt his feet touch sand—but not to walk, for a giant comber swept him shoreward, half buffeting the life out of his half-frozen body. Stumbling, crawling through the small surf in the dark, he at last came to dry sand,

RICHARD FALCONER

where he fell and lay utterly exhausted, to sink into a coma-like sleep. When he awoke it was daylight, and his first conscious thought was the query, "Where am I?" On a sandbank he could not survive a single day in the tropical sun. His eyes were full of sand and gummy with salt water, and it was some time before he could see clearly. And what a relief to find vegetation—green bushes behind him, and other small islands in the offing! Later, when he realized that the other islands were no more than low, sandy islets and that his own refuge was little better—there being no trees whatever—

62

hopes of survival left him. But, with a tenacity to life almost paradoxical in the face of what he believed to be his own quick dissolution, he set about searching for food. And note how, faced with implacable necessity, *genus homo* can adapt itself to a rigorous life, and survive what at first sight appears to be insurmountable obstacles. After surviving the ordeal of several hours in the sea he is saved by a miracle, only to find that he has exchanged the frying-pan for the fire. On this tiny, treeless isle, too small to harbour wild animals that might have provided him meat, and without wells, springs, or running fresh water, the chances of survival were negligible. But let us watch how this sailor sets about the business of keeping body and soul together.

First he searched the island, not a difficult matter, since it was no more than two miles across in its greatest diameter. Walking through the bushes, he was not long in discovering that it was inhabited by rats and sea birds, the latter laying their eggs in the sand. Here and there he came upon an egg, and if it was not too addled he swallowed the contents raw. Such was his first meal. The next need was water, but this was not so easy. The brazen sun, climbing to its zenith, beat down upon him till his thirst became well-nigh insupportable. Night brought some relief, but on the second day, in that heat, unless he drank he must go mad. In the end he was driven to the unpleasant extremity of drinking his own urine, and for two days more he held off madness and death by surrendering to this last resort of the desperate. Now he seriously thought of suicide, for even this disgusting and unnatural substitute could not be for ever continued. A curious fear prevented his suicide; not the fear of death, but horror at the idea of the rats afterward devouring him. The eggs he continued to find and eat were now impossible to swallow owing to his parched and swollen tongue. But he was saved by the capture of a booby, which he knocked over with a stick as it sat perched on a bush. The booby, as many castaways have found out, is not a difficult bird to catch, especially in virgin places of the earth where predatory man has not appeared before.

The bird's warm blood somewhat assuaged Falconer's terrible thirst, and so enabled him to swallow the raw flesh, which he tore off with as little squeamishness as a hungry wild cat. Now he made the discovery that the boobies did not belie their name. With reasonable cunning they could be easily knocked over, and thereafter he caught many of the unsuspecting fowl. Good or bad events seldom come singly, and it was so now. A rain squall descended on the island shortly after the capture of the first booby, and the next day the castaway found cavities in the rocks brimming with fresh water. To preserve the water from evaporation by the sun he scraped under a bush,[1] with his hands and a stick, a deep hole, which was lined with mud and stones stamped down hard. Lacking a receptacle in which to carry the water from the rock crannies to the well, he would soak his shirt in the water, and thus convey it across to the hole, where it was squeezed out. The waterhole he called his 'reservoir.' Two days were required to fill the reservoir. Taking heart at his success with the birds and the discovery of water, he decided to try to produce a fire by the ancient method of sticks and friction. Aided by the heat and the dryness of everything, this was not difficult, and before long he was broiling his boobies on a stick over an open fire. The process of adaptation was proceeding nicely. The housing trouble was not yet solved, but he made good shift by lying snug in a hollow under a Burton wood bush at nights and during the day while the sun was high. The nights were cold, and his cotton shirt, waistcoat and breeches, thread stockings, and thin shoes were insufficient to keep him warm, though more than sufficient during the day.

Sartorially, his greatest regret was the lack of a hat of some sort. The dangerous tropical sun brought on head-aches, and he suffered from incipient sunstroke, though, as

---

[1] These bushes were known to the logwood men as Burton wood.

previously stated, during the hottest hours he stayed under the shade of the bushes, and covered his head and body with leaves. Later on he made a *wooden* cap of green sprigs lined with the sleeves torn from his shirt!

He tried constructing a cupboard of dried mud, by mixing earth and water, in order to have somewhere to store the carcasses of the boobies he had killed and broiled. The 'cupboard' was four feet long by three high and two deep, and was quite an ingenious affair, until the hot sun reduced it to dust and brought about its collapse. This was a more serious misfortune than it might at once appear, since the forty odd birds that he had broiled would not keep long in such a climate. One of his greatest deprivations was the lack of any kind of container. An old rusty iron pot would have been a godsend—a big step forward in the amelioration of his wretchedness.

So a month passed—as near as could be guessed—during the whole of which time he had subsisted on boobies and their eggs. His skin was burnt as though stained with wal-nut, and his clothing was rapidly becoming a costume of picturesque rags. He still possessed the worn volume of Ovid which he had been reading in the boat, and which he had since almost committed to memory through constant reading. But even the Latin poet began to pall, and Falconer's mind turned more and more inward. He spent hours immobile on the sand, morosely brooding on his mis-fortune. Was he doomed to remain alone until he perished for the rats to devour his skeleton carcass? Would he soon lose the power of speech? The thought worried him greatly, and he would purposely hold conversations with himself, as though there were two people instead of one. The position was incomparably worse than that of Crusoe or Selkirk, and unless a timely ship arrived he could not survive long. But a ship did, of course, arrive, though not perhaps in the manner one would choose if one could so order these things.

Some time early in November, while lying crouched under a bush for shelter against the driving sand and wind from a heavy gale, he saw, out to sea, a vessel in distress. She was fast driving on a lee-shore, and even as he watched she struck at a point about a quarter of a mile away. Friend or enemy, it mattered not to Falconer. Running excitedly to the spot, he found four men busy salving what stores they could from their vessel, which lay on her bilge in the

breakers. He hailed them in English, in which language they replied. His joy at seeing them was somewhat greater than their joy at being on this barren coast. Now, for the first time, he learned that he was on one of the Alcranes, a group of five islets, little more than sandbanks, and sixty miles from Campeachy, on the Main.

Falconer and his four 'guests' worked hard salvaging stores from the wreck, and soon had stacked high up on the beach, beyond the reach of the sea, half a dozen barrels of beef, half as many of pork, two each of flour and pease, eleven kegs of biscuit, also rum, brandy, a chest of sugar, a small iron pot, some clothes, and a fowling-piece, with the necessary horn of powder and shot. The clothes were specially retrieved for Falconer, whose own garments would have shamed a scarecrow. A sail was also brought in, and with this a respectable tent was set up. Falconer, as host, was happier than his newly arrived guests. He now had friends, clothes, food, and shelter, after living for a month alone and shelterless.

The sloop lay firmly wedged in the sand fifty yards from the shore at high water, and when the weather cleared Falconer decided to sleep in the cabin. The others had no objection, and so he made himself comfortable in one of the empty berths aft. His four companions were honest sea-

men, their names being Thomas Randall, of Cork, Richard White, of Port Royal, William Musgrave, of Kingston, and Ralph Middleton, of Cowes, Isle of Wight. With four others they had sailed from Port Royal for Campeachy on a trading voyage, but in a quarrel with the Indians and Spaniards there four of the Englishmen were killed, and the survivors were on their way back to Jamaica when they were cast ashore on this spot, which Falconer had long since dubbed Makeshift Island.

Wrecks have often proved useful to castaways; the very fabric which throws them ashore destitute may later befriend them, and this one was no exception. From planking and empty casks a raft was fashioned, from which the castaways would angle. In this way many fish were caught, including a shark.

Here the original narrative is broken by a long sermon

from Falconer, beginning with a lamentation on his own sorry fate (for one so young as he) and followed by a speech from one of the sailors, who points out the ameliorating circumstances: how their fate could be so much worse, and how it behoved them to be grateful for such mercies as had been vouchsafed them. Affairs could be far worse; the sloop was undamaged, and with an effort she might be floated again. After suggesting a plan for getting her off the sand he drifts into a long story of shipwreck, of how he was once cast on a rock in the Baltic—a diverting tale, the

moral of which hinted at fortitude and perseverance overcoming all difficulties. From this he goes on to relate a blood-curdling story of an adventure with the Indians, and ends up with the words addressed to our hero: "Now think yourself, Mr Falconer, whether we need doubt the Providence of God in helping us from this Island."

This long speech, illustrated by a moral, had the desired stiffening effect, and the next morning, after prayers beseeching the assistance of the Almighty, the five men set to work to clear the sand from under the sloop's bilges. For sixteen days they toiled, resting only on Sundays, and had cleared away so much sand as to allow poles to be thrust beneath the keel. But before the sloop could be heaved into deep water one of the men, Thomas Randall, fell ill with some sort of fever, and after a few days died. Before passing away he moralizes at some length to the others on his approaching dissolution. The rest, seeing his case to be hopeless, prayed for his speedy release. He was sewn up in a hammock and buried in the sand. Falconer took charge of a dog left by its late master, and the poor animal had to be tied up to prevent its scratching up the shallow grave.

On Monday, December 31, the sloop, after being stored with provisions, and new rigging set up, was successfully got afloat, and moored with two anchors close to the beach. That night a celebration was held on board in anticipation

of their imminent deliverance. Rum kegs were broached, and all four men got most deplorably drunk. Somehow the three remaining men, who still slept ashore, managed to get safely back to their tent, leaving Falconer to spend the night as usual in the cabin. Since the ways of the men ashore and Falconer on the ship now diverge for a time we will turn our attention to the latter. When he awoke from his rummy sleep it was daylight, and he felt the deck rising and falling with the movement of the sloop. Mounting the ladder to find out the reason, he was staggered to discover the sloop at sea, with the island nowhere in sight. So great was the shock of this discovery that he fell on deck in a swoon. On reviving he began to reflect upon the evils of strong drink, and vented his grief in a torrent of words and tears. Such fatal carelessness! *Primo*, if only the sloop had been more securely moored! *Secondo*, if he had not been stupefied by liquor he would have wakened at the first motion of the vessel, and would in all probability have been able to keep her from blowing out to sea. The punch which had been their undoing was potent, one bottle of lime juice to a gallon of rum. His first thoughts were for his own lamentable condition, with no sails and no compass, which was still ashore on the island, though of food there was plenty. Then he began to feel uneasy lest his marooned companions should misjudge him, suspecting him of deserting them.

For two weeks the sloop drifted at the mercy of fair winds and currents, while, fortunately for the lone sailor, the weather remained fine. About the only noteworthy thing he seems to have done during this barren fortnight was to find in the cabin an old glove stuffed with pieces-of-eight, to the number of seventy-five, which he prudently sewed into his waist-band, on the principle that if he survived he might need them. On January 21 he sighted land six leagues to the south-west, which he recognized as Yucatan. Nine days later he drifted into the Bay of Campeachy (as it proved to be). Here he was met by a canoe full of not unfriendly Indians, who took him to the Spanish Governor. Expecting to be received with the brutality usually credited to the Spanish rulers at that time, he was agreeably surprised to be treated with the greatest courtesy and consideration, even to a feast being given to celebrate his delivery from the sea. The good colonists collected money and fitted out a sloop that he might sail to the rescue of his marooned friends. And as a final act of humanity the Governor freed five English prisoners (held suspected of being pirates) that they might accompany him to man the vessel. As it later turned out, the Governor's suspicions were well founded, and one cannot help but feel that he was glad to get rid of the rascals.

So with Falconer they sailed for the Alcranes, and in spite of the comparative shortness of the traverse the passage took fifteen days. Arriving off the island, Falconer went ashore in a boat, and was greatly upset to see the condition of his friends. They were starving, and almost *in extremis.* William Musgrave, especially, was in a very weak condition, and could not have lived much longer. All these miseries,

says Falconer, may be attributed to the sin of ' drunkenness.' Bitterly they had regretted having carried all their stores into the sloop, for now they were without food. For five days they had neither water nor food of any sort, then one of them thought of the corpse of Thomas Randall. The rest can be imagined. With a tinder-box they started a fire, and parts of the corpse were roasted on sticks, until it had all disappeared.

The starving men were got on board the sloop, and Falconer, as captain, set a course for Jamaica. Of late he had begun to suspect the honesty of his five shipmates. He noticed that they kept together and seemed uncommunicative. He began to feel that the Spanish Governor was probably right in believing them to be pirates. One day he had asked one of them why they had been held by the Spaniards, and had received such a confused and unlikely explanation that he definitely suspected the worst, and confided his suspicions to his rescued friends. Meanwhile the suspected men were plotting to take the ship. They planned first to seize one of their number, Frank Hood, the cook, and kill him if he should make the slightest sound. The plot was to be executed in the next middle watch. Shortly after the first watch was set Falconer heard Warren, one of the mutineers, call for Hood to bring him a can of water as he was " bloody dry." Warren was at that time lying in his hammock below. Falconer crept forward to listen by the scuttle, and heard the ex-pirates discussing their plot. They were to murder Falconer and his friends in their sleep that very night. Some were for delaying the execution of the plan, but the procrastinators were overruled by the masterful Warren, who was all for getting the job done without further delay.

When Hood came on deck Falconer was aware of the cook watching him, and he was glad of the comfort of two pistols he had slipped inside his watch-coat. Hood kept glancing at Falconer until at length, with a look round as though to see that he was not being watched, he stepped up to the captain and said in a low voice, " If you please, Mr Falconer, I have a word to say to you that much concerns you all."

" What is it ? " asked Falconer, keeping the fellow at a distance.

For reply Hood requested the captain to bring his three companions up and he would explain. When they came on deck he indicated that they should retire at a distance from the scuttle to avoid being overheard.

"My companions," he said, " have a wicked design upon you to seize you, put you in the boat, and make off with the ship. I warn you because I think it inhuman." Hearing this, Falconer and his friends decided to seize the mutineers in the third watch. But one of them, distrusting the cook, had listened from behind a bulkhead, and crept forward to advise his companions, who resolved to checkmate their

proposed victims by attacking immediately. The afterguard
in the cabin, waiting for their own zero hour, suddenly
found themselves looking into the wide muzzles of the
mutineers' pistols, and in a trice were securely bound in their
own ship. At dawn their ankles were unbound and they
were taken on deck for exercise. Here Falconer expostulated
with their captors, but, getting no satisfaction, demanded
what they intended to do with them. Warren calmly
answered that he meant to put them in a boat and turn it
adrift, adding, "As for that Hood, we'll murder him without mercy. A dog, to betray us! But as you have not so
much injured us we'll put you immediately in the boat with
a week's provisions and a small sail, and you can seek your
fortune, as I suppose you would have done to us."

To which Falconer answered, "No, we only designed to
confine you till we came to Jamaica, and there to have given
you your liberty. Put us ashore at any land belonging to
the English and we will not think that you have done us an
injury."

But, being a liar himself, Warren was not disposed to
believe that Falconer would have been so clement had he
been the victor, and he impatiently refused to entertain such
a suggestion. The prisoners watched the boat being got
ready, feeling that they were merely being condemned to
a slow and hideous death. They saw put into the boat a
barrel of biscuit, a keg of fresh water, half a dozen pieces
of beef, and a like quantity of pork, and besides these provisions a small kettle, a tinder-box, four cutlasses, and a
fowling-piece, with a few pounds of powder and shot. This
being done, Warren ordered the others to stand by for
Hood's execution, as the leader of the mutineers was firmly
determined that the cook should die for what he called his
treachery. Hood was ordered to be bound to the mast.
Now Warren, goaded by his passion, turned and snatched
the pistol from Falconer's belt, a pistol he believed to be
unloaded, and, savagely loading it, rammed the charge

home. The others begged for the unfortunate Hood's life, but Warren, swearing that nothing could save the bloody dog, cocked the twice-charged pistol, levelled it, and fired at the breast of his victim. There was a deafening report, and Warren, struck in his thick skull by a piece of the exploded pistol, fell dying on the deck. One of the flying pieces of metal grazed the head of Falconer, but he was not hurt. Hood, who had escaped all injury, burst his bonds in his fright, fell down, then, recovering, sprang to the aid of his friends, whom he unbound unnoticed by the other mutineers, who were bending over the prostrate figure of their leader. The doughty cook, feverishly pulling at the knots which bound the arms of his friends, paused for a moment to fell the helmsman, who had left the tiller to come and interfere with the work so gallantly begun. It all happened with the suddenness of a thunder-clap, and within a few minutes the remaining pirates were overpowered by their late victims and fast bound, while Warren dramatically sat up on deck, crossed himself, and repented of his sins before he died. Without ceremony, his body was heaved overboard.

The three remaining pirates asked to be put in the boat and set free, fearing, doubtless, a more violent end, but Falconer, being short-handed, preferred to keep them to help work the ship, and generously promised to free them when they reached Jamaica. Seeing their captors so lenient, they became friendly, and cravenly blamed Warren for the mutiny. The next day the ship was chased and caught by pirates, who, it was discovered, were the friends of the dead Warren and his men. Hearing the story of the abortive mutiny and of Hood's part in it, they tortured this poor fellow, and took off the three men who had such a short time before attempted to ingratiate themselves with Falconer. In exchange for the three scoundrels the pirate leader sent Falconer one man, a fellow too ill with fever to be of any use.

RICHARD FALCONER

Once more Falconer is wrecked, this time on the Spanish Main, where he is for the second time graciously entertained by the Spaniards. But his Crusoe adventure is over, and we leave him on board a ship beating into the entrance to the Channel in July 1700.

CHAPTER IV

The Terrible Experiences of Fourteen Men
on Boon Island

THE Crusoes of fiction are almost invariably cast upon tropical or semi-tropical isles, where the sand is white and the waving fronds of palm throw cool, green shadows on the luxuriant undergrowth. But, as like as not, the Crusoes of fact find themselves on rocky islets, where the wind pierces to the very marrow and vegetation is non-existent. In the winter months Boon Island, twenty-one miles off the mouth of the Piscataqua[1] river, between the states of Maine and New Hampshire, approaches this condition. To be marooned there in this year of grace would not entail any hardship, but two hundred odd years ago Boon Island was as remote from civilization as North Greenland is to-day.

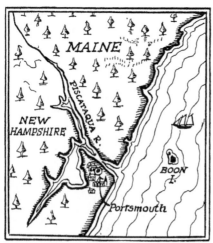

On September 25, 1710, the *Nottingham*, galley, 120 tons and ten

[1] Pronounced Piskataw-qua.

guns, with a crew of fourteen under Captain John Dean, left
England for Boston, then a small town, but growing rapidly
with the flow of emigrants from the British Isles. After an
irksome passage, due to contrary winds, the *Nottingham* raised
the land opposite the Piscataqua river early in December in
a driving blizzard which made visibility so poor that Captain
Dean proceeded with the utmost circumspection.

On the night of December 11, between 8 and 9 P.M.,
while groping through the blinding snow and sleet, the
crew was startled by the sight of a white line of breakers

directly ahead. Though the helm was instantly put over,
before the rudder could swing the bows round the ship
struck with terrific force, and began to smash herself to
pieces upon the unseen rocks. The night was black as a
cave, and nothing could be seen of the land. It might be
close aboard or a mile away, and as a full gale was blowing it
appeared impossible that any of the men could escape from
the deadly trap they had been caught in. Believing that the
end was but a matter of minutes, all hands went into the
cabin, where they fell on their knees supplicating the mercy
of Providence. But the captain, being a practical man, and
deciding that prayers would be of more use if aided by personal effort, ordered the men on deck to cut the masts, in
the forlorn hope that thus the ship might be saved, at least
until the crew could get ashore. As the wind was blowing
on the land, when the weather shrouds were severed the
masts fell shoreward. One of the crew, peering through

77

the murk from the end of the bowsprit, shouted that he could just make out a group of rocks thirty or forty yards away, and if another would accompany him he would

attempt to reach them. Captain Dean thereupon requested the best swimmers to try to gain the rocks, and to shout out if successful. After giving them ample time to get across, and hearing no shouts from the rocks, those on the wreck concluded that the unfortunate volunteers had been drowned.

Remembering certain papers of value, the captain attempted to descend into the cabin to retrieve them, also to secure, if possible, a bottle of brandy, some ammunition, and a purse of money; but, finding the cabin full of water, he had to abandon the idea. Now this Captain John Dean, who, like another seafaring man of the same name,[1] was a redoubtable fellow, stripped to his underclothes and jumped

into the icy water, determined to reach the rock or perish in the effort. Bruised and lacerated against the jagged granite, he clung like a limpet to the sides of the dark mass, until he could summon sufficient strength to haul himself to the top. In the darkness he heard voices, and presently made out the forms of the first volunteers, who were alive, but unable to make their half-paralysed throats utter cries loud enough to be heard above the gale. Now others came, until the entire company had assembled on the exposed refuge of the rock. All attempts to crawl round to the

[1] See *The Indian Ocean*, Chapter IV, by the present author.

lee-side failed, owing to its slippery and precipitous flanks, and the wet and half-frozen men had to sit huddled together, suffering agonies from the wind and snow, till daybreak, when it was seen that they were on an island, and not a spur of rock as they had believed. Floating in the surf were spars, cable, pieces of timber, and planks, but no casks which might contain food. Scrambling down the rocks to the narrow shore, they picked up a few pieces of sodden cheese, which provided the only food that day. Before nightfall a

shelter of spars and torn canvas had been set up on a level spot, and into this the miserable company crawled, and lay as close together as possible throughout the second wretched night. An effort had been made to produce fire with steel and flint on a piece of rag, but this was abandoned owing to the rag being damp. For eight or ten days the men persevered in their efforts to obtain fire, and, not succeeding, gave it up for good.

The second day, the weather clearing, the mainland, seven leagues to the west, could be faintly seen, and a plan to build a boat was discussed. Captain Dean ordered every man who was able to search the rocks for timber and anything which might serve as material or tools with which to build the proposed boat. But some of the crew lay too ill with cold and hunger to be of any assistance to their shipmates. The worst of the sick cases, the cook, died at midday, and the body was placed at the edge of the water for the waves to carry away. Afterward, when hunger had rendered them less squeamish, most of the men confessed that when the cook had died they had looked hungrily at the corpse, but had been ashamed to voice what was in their minds. After three days on the island the weather increased in severity, and every one began to suffer from frost-bite, hands and feet turning ominously white. When shoes and socks were pulled off pieces of skin, and even the toe-nails, would come with them. The men were in mortal fear of gangrene, and did what they could to restore warmth by

wrapping their feet and legs in canvas and oakum. In this respect the more active ones were the better off, and found that an ounce of exercise was worth a pound of swaddling.

The first crude shelter was soon abandoned for a stronger and more wind-proof affair, pyramidal in form, with sides eight feet long of sails that had driven ashore. Space within was so limited that there was just room to lie at full length, though no one could turn unless all turned, this being done by agreement every two hours throughout the night. As it was found impossible to construct a conventionally shaped boat, a box-like punt was begun, but with such crude tools and limited material available even this was a disheartening task. A saw was fashioned from the blade of a cutlass notched by hacking with sheath knives. A caulking mallet, a hammer, and a number of nails had already been picked up among the rocks. More nails were drawn from the sheathing of the wreck. Three planks were taken for the bottom, two more of similar length for the sides, and two shorter pieces for the ends. To raise the sides a sort of 'dodger' of Holland duck was fastened on short stanchions. The 'boat' was caulked with strips of canvas and oakum picked from an old cable. Some pieces of sheet lead and leather were found useful to cover the more blatant gaps. Into this shallow box a short mast was stepped and rigged with a square sail, and seven paddles were roughly fashioned, one longer than the rest for a steering oar. The carpenter, their most-needed man at this time, was too ill to be of much use, and the entire work had fallen on the only three sound men on the island. The rest crawled or lay about in varying degrees of numbness, and for days at a time the entire company would be forced by the rigorous New England weather to remain confined within the little tent. The same New England cold which admits of such delightful snow-shoeing, ski-ing, skating, and ice-boating was nearly the death of all the wretched men on Boon Island.

A week after the wreck, during which time the only food to pass their lips had been pieces of sodden cheese and a few crunched bones, three boats were seen about five leagues distant. At such a grand sight there was much premature rejoicing, and the captain made all the men crawl out and shout together, the sum total of this croaking chorus being about equivalent to the cry of an owl heard in a distant wood. When the boats had disappeared the dejected men crawled back into their shelter to lie brooding in silence, a few being buoyed with the hope that a piece of the wreck might drift on to the mainland and so bring assistance. Before the boat was finished the carpenter's axe was washed ashore, and this was regarded as a godsend. The work was now greatly facilitated, and on December 21, ten days after being wrecked, they painfully dragged the unstable little craft into the water. As the sea was calm and the sky clear it was decided to set off at once, the captain to take with him the strongest men, who were the mate, the skipper's brother, and four others. No sooner had they all got in than a big roller caught the craft, and threw it ashore, smashing to pieces a week's desperate labour, and nearly drowning the crew. And, what was worse, the precious axe and hammer were lost. With this calamity went all hope of reaching the main by their own exertions. But when an hour or so later a gale blew up the disappointed men saw how the boat's crew had been saved from a worse calamity. Better lose the boat on the beach than while at sea. Had

they been caught by the gale while in their shallow box offshore nothing could have saved them.

The captain was now the only sound man; most of the others' hands and feet were obviously mortifying, and even should they live the worst cases must expect amputation. Their legs were bitten with deep ulcers, which, through the lack of means of dressing them, made the tent almost unbearable for the others. Wretchedness could scarcely go farther; there was no fire, and no food save scanty bits of the unappetizing rockweed and a few mussels, at the most two or three a day apiece. Starvation was daily drawing closer, and there seemed to the most sanguine no longer any hope. Furthermore, they believed that the spring tides would cover the rock even should they survive so long.

Most of the men had resigned themselves, and avowed their willingness to die. But so lightly are such vows meant that when the mate had the good fortune to strike down a rash sea-gull every one was grateful for the morsel of meat the bird provided.

Among those who were badly frost-bitten was a stout fellow who had lost the use of both feet, a Swede, whose name I regret not being able to record. For this Swede was a *man*. He suggested that they should build a raft with what wood could be found, and he, being of no use to the others, would attempt with one volunteer to get across to the main for succour. At first the idea was rejected as impossible, but the Swede's persuasions prevailed, and with practically no tools work was begun on the construction of the raft. Its two main longitudinals were the two halves of the split foreyard, each twelve feet long, with other odd lengths of spars between, the whole bound together and covered with light planks, lashed and nailed. From a short staff two hammocks were bent to make a small rag of a sail, and a paddle was made for each man, with one to spare. When it was finished the Swede asked Captain Dean if he wished to go, giving him to understand that if he declined there were two other men ready to embrace the opportunity. Better death than this wretched inactivity, which would end in death anyway. While they were talking a boat was seen in the distance off the mouth of the Piscataqua, a sight which made the Swede more than ever eager to quit the thrice-damned rock. But as the sea was then far too rough for a safe embarkation, let alone a safe passage to the main, the departure of the raft had to be put off until the following day, Captain Dean having meanwhile decided for good reasons to remain behind with the men. Further work on the raft delayed its readiness until late in the afternoon, when the captain stepped forward and opposed its launching on the grounds of the lateness of the hour and the risk of making the passage in the dark. But the Swede and his one companion begged to be allowed to depart at once, pointing out that the nights were so light there could be no hazard on the score of darkness. Seeing their pathetic eagerness to make the attempt, the master gave his consent, and the two men, accompanied by such as were able to hobble or crawl, went down to the water's edge to the raft. Wading deep and climbing on, they pushed out to the first breakers. But in their feeble state they were unable to keep the craft

head on to the breaking combers, and the story of the boat was repeated. The curling wall of water slewed the raft round, and men, oars, and raft were thrown violently in a whirling, tumbling confusion back toward the land. The Swede swam ashore unaided, but his companion had to be rescued by the captain, who was the only man with strength enough left to do it. The rescued man, too full of salt water to have any stomach for another attempt, retired, and, seeing how things were, the captain requested the Swede to assist him in dragging the raft out of the water, and to await a more favourable time before making another attempt. Though unable to stand, the indomitable Swede

85

persisted in his resolution to go, and, kneeling on a rock, gripped the captain's hands, beseeching him to come along with him. "I am certain to die here," he said, "but there is a chance that I may be the means of bringing succour to you and the rest of the men. But if you refuse to go I am determined to make the attempt myself, even if I have to go alone, for I am resolutely bent on this venture." Not waiting for the captain's answer, he begged him to aid in turning the raft and help him upon it.

Captain Dean, though sympathizing, believed that the attempt would be equivalent to suicide, especially now that the mast and sail were gone, and tried to dissuade the Swede from his purpose. But the latter insisted that he would rather perish in the sea than remain another day in such a wretched state. Hearing this, one of the listening company came forward, and offered to go. The Swede was overjoyed at this sudden development, and hobbled to the raft, which was once more got afloat. This time, with his new ship-mate, or raftmate, he got safely through the breakers, and by sunset they had become a tiny dark speck out on the water between the rock and the main. They were judged to be then half-way, and with good luck on their side might conceivably reach the coast about two in the morning.

But this was not to be their good fortune, for they were never seen alive again, though afterward the raft was found on the beach near the Piscataqua river, and a mile away the corpse of the second man, with a paddle fastened to his wrist. The body of the Swede was never recovered.

Four days they waited, those on the island, before losing hope. Once a column of smoke rising from above the woods on the mainland was thought to be a signal, but nothing came of it, and the despairing men lapsed back into apathy. The spring tides were past; danger from that source was over, but the knowledge was of small consolation. Death by slow starvation seemed inevitable. The captain's stomach had at last revolted against the eternal rockweed, though he continued to gather it for the others. Being the strongest of the party, it was left to him to find the greater part of the food — rockweed and mussels — with the result that through constant immersion his hands and arms got into a terrible state, and were in serious danger. Better food than the revolting rockweed and mussels was for ever in sight, but, Tantalus-like, not within reach. There were seals, but these creatures felt no altruism toward the starving men, and kept well beyond reach of Captain Dean, who attempted stalking them with a club. There were gulls too, thousands of them, but no less shy than the seals. The only acceptable element there seemed to be abundance of was water, rain- and snow-water, which was drunk from an empty powder-horn.

One day a piece of leather, found nailed to the mainyard, which had drifted ashore, was cut up into thin pieces and greedily swallowed. The mussels and rockweed were growing scarcer, and the weaker men had sunk into a state of permanent invalidism. They lay in the tent all day, waited upon by those who could crawl about. The condition of even the strongest was unspeakably wretched, living as they were in quarters a dog would turn away from. The tent had become so wet within and without that an attempt, only partially successful, was made at thatching the top with strands of oakum from the untwisted main cable. This would keep off the rain for two or three hours until the saturation point was reached, and then the tent became as wet as ever. The oakum also served the purpose of wrapping round their bodies after they had shed their sodden clothes at night. But these conditions could not go on indefinitely, and toward the end of December, the carpenter, who had been ill so long, died. Aged forty-seven, a corpulent, phlegmatic man, he had complained of stiffness in the neck and back, with excessive pain; he had lain for days quite helpless. It was seen that he had but a few hours to live, and in the night, while they prayed for his soul, he quietly died. But because of their weakness and the cold outside the body was allowed to remain among them all night, so close, indeed, that one unfortunate man lay pressed against it.

In the morning, as the captain left to go on his usual search for mussels and rockweed, he asked the two strongest to remove the carpenter's body from the tent. After a protracted and disheartening search for the miserable sustenance he so hated he returned to his companions, and found the body still in the tent among them. Demanding to know why it had not been removed, he received the lethargic answer that they were too weak to do so. Captain Dean said nothing, but, taking a piece of rope, fastened it round the body, and with some reluctant assistance from the stronger ones dragged it outside, some distance beyond the tent. But the exertion had been almost too much for him, for he crawled back to the tent in a fainting condition. The men, seeing their resolute and pious-minded leader thus, judged the moment propitious to voice what was in their minds. They pleaded with him to be allowed to eat part of the dead carpenter's body. Three weeks previously they had been a company of average normal men, who, doubtless, would have been as shocked at the idea of cannibalism among white men as you or I. They were in a well-found ship with full bellies and stout hearts. But within three weeks they had come to this—proposing to eat the body of their dead shipmate. The captain was no less shocked at the suggestion than any honest man would be, and was not at first disposed to hear of such an unnatural act. He reflected in silence for a long time on the morals of the deed, but his ultimate acquiescence was no doubt influenced by his own stomach's craving. He afterward frankly confessed that "conscience and other considerations were obliged to submit to the more prevailing arguments of our craving appetite."

So the decision was made, and, once having decided, the

men were in danger of losing all self-restraint and falling upon the unwholesome corpse like wild beasts. To make the doubtful ethics of the business as decent as possible, to preserve some of his self-respect, the captain ordered that the skin, feet, hands, head, and bowels should be cast into the sea before anyone ate a morsel of the flesh.

Now the men, who seemed to have become like children pitifully dependent upon a stronger creature, complained that they had not the strength to cut up the body, and requested the captain to perform this grisly work. With what reluctance he carried it out we can fairly guess, for the captain was a humane man. The butchery was not completed till nightfall.

Here let me digress a moment. Once, referring to a former book of mine,[1] a critic deplored a certain squeamishness (so he named it) in omitting the details of a similar butchery of a dead body by a boatload of famished sailors. Perhaps it is a piece of literary cowardice, and not, as we like to think, a fine sense of delicacy that makes us pass over scenes of cannibalism and similar unpleasant things.

Then shall I describe how the dead torso was cut into thin and succulent slices, washed in salt water, and eaten, on the advice of the captain, with a dessert of rockweed? Our captain was a realist; he describes in great detail how he ate this unique food, what it tasted and chewed like, and finally—maybe as a sop to our sensibilities—how his stomach revolted at it, as it had revolted against the tough and unappetizing rockweed. At the first banquet the mate and two others refused to join in, but the next morning this trio succumbed to hunger and took a share with the rest. Every one ate so greedily that the captain was constrained to remove what remained of the flesh to a niche in a craggy rock beyond reach, lest his companions should injure themselves by over-eating. Nor had he overlooked the necessity of making the remains last as long as possible by doling them

[1] *Ships and Sailors.*

out in small portions. Among eleven men the body of the carpenter would not go far. Fortunately this man, whose wisdom and strength of purpose undoubtedly kept his companions from lapsing into utter savagery and degeneration, still possessed the physical superiority to enforce his rule. He determined to make the remains last as long as humanly possible, as he feared that when the body had gone the men would murder one of themselves for the sake of the food they must have. Describing the men at this time, the captain afterward wrote:

> . . . in a few days, I found their very natural dispositions changed; and that affectionate, peaceable temper they had hitherto displayed altogether lost. Their eyes were wild and staring, their countenances fierce and barbarous, and instead of obeying my commands, as they had universally and readily done before, I found that all I could say, and even prayers and entreaties, were vain and fruitless. Nothing was now to be heard but brutish quarrels, instead of that quiet, submissive spirit of prayer and supplication which we had previously enjoyed. Nor were these the only evils, for the ulceration of the people became worse, from feeding on human flesh; and I suffered equally in this respect.

This, however, was the darkest hour before the dawn, for on the morning of January 2, when he crawled out of the tent to fetch a portion of meat from the rock, Captain Dean saw a shallop[1] standing toward the island. In his weakened condition, with nerves frayed to a thin edge, he was nearly beside himself with excitement and the reaction; nor were the others any less affected. They watched the shallop approach within a hundred yards of the breakers and drop anchor, obviously prevented from approaching closer by the heavy south-west swell. The vessel remained off-shore all the morning, waiting for smoother water with the flood tide.

The arrival of the sloop was no mere accident. The

[1] A small sailing craft long since obsolete.

castaways learned later how the finding of the raft and the dead body of the Swede's companion had aroused the suspicions of the people on the coast, and they had come out expressly to investigate. So the sacrifice had not been in vain.

Captain Dean, standing at the edge of the surf and shouting across to the people in the shallop, told them the story of the shipwreck and the sufferings of himself and his companions, only withholding any reference to their starvation for fear that the visitors might refuse to risk coming ashore lest they should be forced to remain by bad weather in such a dreadful place, sharing the miserable fate of those already there. Continuing to shout across the intervening stretch of water, the captain earnestly pleaded for the immediate release of the castaways, or, if that were impossible, at least for the means of obtaining a fire. Yielding to the latter request, a man left the shallop in a canoe, and after nearly losing his life in the breakers made the shore, utterly exhausted. When he had somewhat recovered he showed his astonishment at the wasted condition of the castaways, but, seeing the scraps of flesh lying on the ledge of rock, quickly remarked that at any rate they could not be entirely destitute. At this the captain, who remained spokesman for the rest, forced himself to admit that the man was right, still fearing the consequences of the truth. With some difficulty a fire was made, and every one got as close to it as possible for the heartening warmth it gave out. In the afternoon the captain attempted to go off to the shallop with the visitor, but the surf overturned the canoe at once, and the captain, on account of his feeble condition, was nearly drowned before he could be hauled out of the water. The visitor, however, was able to succeed alone, after promising to return the next day.

But that night another of the interminable succession of gales blew up, and the visitors lost their shallop on the main, and barely escaped with their lives. Again the castaways had escaped an ill wind that, in their weakened state, would surely have drowned them all. Swimming ashore, the wrecked shallop's crew sent messages to Portsmouth[1] for assistance.

Meanwhile another little drama was being played out on Boon Island. The men's gloom at the departure of the shallop was somewhat assuaged by the presence of a fire, by which they could not only warm their chilled bodies, but broil their meat. But this proved to be a doubtful blessing, for the fire, composed of short lengths of frayed rope laid on a flat stone, made such a smoke in the tent where it was placed that at first every one was violently sick, even to fainting.

The next day the gale continued, and no vessel appeared, but the captain decided to risk allowing all hands an extra ration of the meat, a concession that had the effect of causing every one to demand more. During the ensuing night, when the men were all lying in the tent, presumably asleep, Captain Dean heard two of them whispering, planning to steal and eat part of the meat while their comrades slept.

Deciding to wait before taking any action, the captain lay pretending to be asleep while one of the thieves returned with a piece of the flesh. Waiting until they were in the act of broiling it over the embers of the fire, the captain started up, seized the piece of flesh, and aroused the rest of the company. When the others saw the evidence of this piece of selfishness their fury made the thieves tremble with fear. A discussion was held to decide how to punish the pair, but when it came to the point of deciding they were forced to admit that not a man among them possessed the strength to carry out such punishment as seemed appropriate. They therefore, rather lamely, decided to administer a severe reprimand instead.

During the day the remainder of the body was eaten, and

[1] In New Hampshire.

unless aid came quickly the more atavistic of the men might
commit some shocking act for the sake of appeasing their
maddening hunger. That night the gale abated, and at
daybreak the sound of a musket-shot brought every one to
the opening of the tent. There, in the half-light of early

dawn, could be seen a fair-sized sloop. In it were five men,
two of them coasting captains. They had on board a large
canoe, which they lost no time in sending ashore. Within
two hours of first seeing the sloop all the castaways were on
board her. Being unable to walk, they had been carried to
the canoe on the backs of their rescuers, who took them off
two at a time. On board the sloop they were given morsels

93

of bread and a swallow of rum, but for a time were unable to retain even this small amount of spirits. While the sloop lay off-shore two other vessels came in, but their services were not needed, and the little fleet returned triumphantly to the main, bearing the chief actors in one of the most remarkable and most melancholy tragedies that had ever happened on the New England coast.

At eight in the evening the castaways were taken ashore, and received in the home of one of the settlers, a stark enough place in the New England of 1710, with its virgin forests, vast acres of wilderness, and hostile Indians, but doubtless a heaven on earth to the eleven resurrected castaways. In the farmer's house they were nursed back to health, every man surviving, albeit minus a few fingers or toes, and a youth, an apprentice, losing the greater part of a foot—all from frost-bite. Before antiseptic surgery, such recoveries were something in the nature of a miracle.

As for Captain Dean, he went to sea again, but in his later years settled on shore to become British Consul for the Flanders ports, and, residing at Ostend, died there in 1761.

CHAPTER V

Cast Ashore on Patagonia

To wake each joyless morn, and search again
　　The famish'd haunts of solitary men;
Whose race, unyielding as their native storm,
　　Knows not a trace of nature; but the form.
　　　Yet, at thy call, the hardy tar pursued,
Pale but intrepid—sad, but unsubdued;
　　Pierced the deep woods, and hailing from afar
　　　The moon's pale planet and the northern star,
Paus'd at each dreary cry unheard before,
　　Hyenas in the wild, and mermaids on the shore.

THOMAS CAMPBELL, *The Pleasures of Hope*

WHETHER there were hyenas and mermaids in Patagonia or not does not much matter, since the adventures of the shipwrecked castaways of the *Wager* were quite comparable with that of meeting a hyena or a mermaid. Those former-day ballad-mongers who sat at home and wrote theatrical doggerel about some fantastically imagined land may readily be forgiven their ignorance. Two hundred, one hundred, years ago Patagonia was still practically a *terra incognita*. Some people still believed that it was a country of giants, and Tierra del Fuego was accepted literally as a land of fire where presumably only salamanders could exist. But are we moderns the better for our knowledge, for losing the charm of mystery that once enveloped the whole earth? How satisfying to imagine Patagonia to be inhabited by giants, mermaids, and hyenas! Or to believe that in the Everglades of Florida was to be found

95

the Fountain of Youth, or in the existence of Inca cities of virgin gold! And how barren the world becomes as we are disillusioned!

All of which is germane to this thought—the thought that these castaway tales are really tales of disillusion. The distant blue peaks are not so blue when they are approached closer. Your picturesque, rocky, sea-girt isle, so inspiring to poets and painters, is less attractive to the castaway, *sans*

food, *sans* shelter, *sans* clothing, than to us stay-at-homes, reading about it, and feeling pleasant shivers up and down our spines as we read of him spending the night perished with cold, clinging to an inhospitable rock.

And so, with Lieutenant Byron of our present tale, the Cordilleras, looking so majestic and so beautiful from the sea, were a positive curse at closer acquaintance. No cannibalism enters into this narrative, as has so frequently happened in Crusoe records, but even without that culminating horror this story of the *Wager's* men is one of the most harrowing and melancholy epics of hardship that has ever been preserved. And when we have read it we cannot help but be impressed (or a little disappointed, if we are of a cynical turn of mind) at the extraordinary tenacity that *genus homo* has of life. He

96

will suffer unspeakable wretchedness merely that he may live. Long after he has anything to live for—except to be alive— he clings to his poor bones.

The chief actor in our present narrative is the Honourable John Byron, at that time lieutenant in the Royal Navy, and of the comparatively tender age of eighteen, although, as the saying goes, old beyond his years. Young Byron, the second son of William, fourth Lord Byron, was born in 1723, and entered the Navy as midshipman, in the usual way, at the astonishingly early age of eight. We can well believe that ten years later, when our narrative begins, he was old for his age. Nor would his subsequent terrible experiences make him any younger. He served forty-five years in the Navy, became Vice-Admiral of the White, and died in 1786, aged sixty-three. It may be of some additional interest to know that he was the grandfather of Lord Byron, the poet.

The *Wager*, Lieutenant Byron's ship, was one of Commodore George Anson's squadron, which left Spithead in September 1740 on the famous expedition to harass Spanish trade in the South Seas. Of all the old crocks Anson had under his command the little *Wager* was the least seaworthy and the least effective as a fighting unit. She was, in fact, an old East Indiaman fitted out as a man-of-war, and manned by a pressed crew. With some difficulty she kept up with the rest of the squadron until the dreaded Cape Horn was rounded in April of the following year. Here they met unusually severe weather, and for some weeks the *Wager*, now lost to the other ships, battled with the terrific seas and violent winds. With the heavy rolling the mizen-mast carried away, and the carpenter and bos'n set up a jury mast with a stun'sail boom. Then all the chain plates to windward tore out of their fastenings, and with the loosened masts it became unsafe to carry an effective press of canvas. As the ship was still labouring badly the bower anchor was cut away in the hope of easing her. Then the worst possible thing happened: the ship began to drive on a lee-shore, and the end was a mere matter of hours. All efforts to claw off were unavailing, and on May 14 she struck a spur of rock on a small island, a hundred miles north of the Straits of Magellan, at four o'clock in the morning, a bad time, as many of the crew were asleep in their hammocks, a number of them being drowned before they could escape. Those lying helpless in advanced stages of scurvy had no chance at all of escaping.

The *Wager* was at once laid on her beam-ends, where she remained while the sea, breaking on her weather side, hammered her mercilessly on the rocks. With such sudden dislocation of the normal life of the ship men lost their heads and ran amuck, pillaging, raving crazily, and riotously broaching the rum barrels in drunken revolt against discipline. A few kept their heads and assisted the officers to restore some semblance of order. Ignoring, with an almost sublime indifference, the floating corpses around him, the mate, Mr Jones, coolly said, "My friends, let us not be discouraged. Have you never seen a ship among breakers before?" Such a dramatic appeal had a heartening effect on the *fainéants*, and the sober ones rallied round him, though afterward, ashore, he confessed that at that time he had not the slightest hope of surviving. The commander of the *Wager*, Captain Cheap, who was suffering from a dislocated shoulder, due to a fall some days before, was of little use in this extremity. A harsh and selfish man, the discontented and frightened crew now mocked him, refusing sullenly to acknowledge further his authority. And, though Lieutenant Byron puts it on record that while the ship lay in

this position of extreme peril Captain Cheap conducted himself with great courage, afterward, on the island, he proved to be monstrously selfish and lacking in sympathy for his men.

The *Wager* struck at 4 A.M., while it was still dark. At daylight, as soon as the position of the coast could be clearly made out, preparations were begun for getting ashore in the boats. It is remarkable that, notwithstanding the high seas running during the morning, no less than 140 men got safely to land. A few of them preferred to remain on the wreck, and for various reasons, not the least of which being Captain Cheap's loss of prestige, they were allowed to remain on board. Why leave their home, their all, for the frowning hospitality of the wild land before them? Such a forbidding, utterly desolate place could surely offer no chance

99

of life to 150 men or so; there could be neither food nor shelter on this barren coast. And so it was, or nearly so. Chance discovered to the castaways a deserted Indian hut, half ruin, but better than the open skies in such a harsh climate. But for food, an even more pressing need than shelter, they fared not so well. Three pounds of biscuit dust brought in one of the boats had to suffice the entire company that first day. Thereafter some beef casks were got ashore, and gastronomical anxieties were for the nonce removed. In the hut great uneasiness was caused by the

discovery of a number of Indian spears. Quite needlessly, the shipwrecked people dreaded the possibility of being discovered by Indians, though possibly this fear came from the stories and legends of the giant Patagonians which still persisted among the ignorant and credulous. After this discovery no one cared to wander far from the camp, though the officers were anxious to survey the country and consider plans for escape.

The first night three of the sailors—already weakened by scurvy—died in the hut. On the second day most of the party were violently sick, suffering from severe colic pains. This was laid to the biscuit dust, which had been put into a tobacco bag that had not been thoroughly emptied of its original contents. But, since this was eaten with the flesh of a seagull and some bunches of wild celery the men had gathered, the sickness may not have been entirely the fault of the biscuit dust.

The location of the 'camp' was a rocky promontory rising so abruptly from the sea that steps had been chipped out with boarding axes in order to reach the comparatively level summit. This place Byron named Mount Misery— not without reason, for the weather was bitterly cold and stormy, and the men were sullen, mutinous, and ill. But, as the wreck showed signs of completely breaking up, those who had remained on board now desired to come ashore, and after signalling their wishes to the shore-party waited, with truculent impatience, for a boat to be sent out to them, heedless of the risks of launching a boat in the big seas breaking on the rocks. Then, because those on the land, seeing the peril, hesitated about putting a boat off at once, the bravoes on the wreck fired the quarter-deck gun at the hut to teach the laggards ashore a lesson. At this show of aggressiveness an attempt was made to launch the boat, but the seas ran too high, and the shore people were forced to desist for that day.

Furious at the failure, the wild men on the wreck showed their august displeasure by a debauch of wanton destruction, smashing up the cabin furniture and plundering the officers' chests there; finally winding up with a violent quarrel among themselves. The next day, however, it was possible to bring them off, and, though in a truculent humour, they were disarmed on coming ashore by the over-awing resolution of Captain Cheap and Lieutenant Hamilton. One of the worst of the newly arrived men was the bos'n, who was wearing an officer's gold-laced coat over his own tarry clothes. After enduring the man's threatening manner for a short while the captain felled him to the ground, and ordered him to be stripped of his finery.

On the rock a tent had been erected for the pitifully inadequate collection of provisions and liquor brought from the wreck, and to prevent pilfering a strong guard of trusted officers and men stood by them day and night. The Indian hut being too small to house the entire company, a number of men nightly found shelter under the cutter, which had been turned keel upward for that purpose. The incessant rain, coupled with the raw cold, soon rendered the men's condition wretched. The tiny ration from the ship's stores had to be supplemented with limpets and other shellfish collected from the rocks. This daily hunt for food was rendered unspeakably horrible by the livid corpses of dead sailors from the *Wager*, which floated in the surf among the rocks, above which screamed countless sea birds.

Parts of the wreck still remained above water, and from the quarter-deck and fore part of the fo'c'sle some of the more enterprising men fished up stores by hooks lashed to poles thrust down through hatches and scuttles. In this labour they were frequently sickened by the sight of pulpy bodies floating among the flotsam between decks. Suppressing their horror, the living would continue groping among the dead for precious food casks, which when found would be loaded into the tossing boat, and at no little risk got ashore. No wonder, then, that a strong guard was put over these hardly won stores, and that pilfering was punished with great severity. Common safety made this necessary, and no one sympathized with the thief. Some poor fellows, nearly maddened by hunger, lost control of themselves, and descended to acts they would normally have abhorred. One boy had to be forcibly restrained from eating the liver of a mangled corpse which lay among the rocks. Others searched the shore for food at night as well as all day, driven by tormenting hunger. Starvation and other physical hardships continued to keep the men intractable and discontented, making the office of their leaders almost a farce, since the threat of mutiny hung in the air like a miasma.

The longboat still lay in the wreck, and a party was now sent out to attempt to secure this large and valuable boat by cutting away the gunwale of the *Wager*, a difficult operation, seeing that it lay under water. While a number of seamen, led by the carpenter, were thus employed they were startled to see three Indian canoes appear from round a point of rock. When it was observed that the natives were really distrustful and timid of the white men signs of friendship were made to them, and somewhat hesitatingly they approached. On landing they were taken before Captain Cheap, who made them small presents, including a looking-glass, which mystified them greatly. They would look at themselves, and then peep behind the glass to discover if a counterpart of themselves stood there. These people were the Patagonians of the extreme southernmost tip of South America, a small, Mongoloid, straight black-haired race, living in a primitive state comparable with the aboriginals of Australia, and little like the giant race believed by many to inhabit these parts. In spite of the bitter cold they wore practically nothing but a scrap of skin round their waists, men and women alike, and their hair, long and unkempt, hung over their faces in brute-like indifference to appearance or comfort. After trying to converse by signs and giving the castaways all they had, a few shellfish, they departed. To them it was a tremendous event—the coming to the islands of such a large party of white men, and men, moreover, who showed a more friendly disposition than their (the Indians') Spanish masters to the north. And to show appreciation for the trifling gifts they returned two days later with three sheep. But three sheep would not last long among such a large company, and the whites bartered some of their possessions for a few half-wild dogs belonging to the Indians. Nor did these dogs go far among the company, and the general air of discontent soon showed itself again. The men's hunger was aggravated by the continuous cold, which demanded of their bodies more heat than they could produce.

Lieutenant Byron wrote in his journal that he was so sick of the eternal quarrelling that he decided to live in a little shelter by himself.

For my own part, seeing it was the fashion, and liking none of their parties, I built a little hut just big enough for myself and a poor Indian dog I found in the woods.

Captain Cheap's growing unpopularity, due to his uncompromising harshness and lack of sympathy for other sufferers, was graphically illustrated by an attempt on the part of a mutinous faction to blow up his quarters. Only after the train was laid were they dissuaded by the more law-abiding element. About this time ten of the discontented ones, the ten strongest amongst them, got hold of an Indian canoe and paddled away. They were never afterward heard of, and doubtless perished either at sea or among the maze of barren islands in that part of the world. But their loss was counted as a distinct gain for the others, and no one mourned them.

Then Captain Cheap, in a cold rage, committed a blunder that neither his officers nor his men ever forgave. A young midshipman, Mr Cozens, a good fellow when sober but quarrelsome when drunk, became involved, while in the latter state, in a bitter dispute with the purser, whom he threatened with a pistol. Here Captain Cheap came on the scene, and, seeing the midshipman drunkenly flourishing a pistol, drew his own and shot him through the body. He fell to the sand, dying, and the angry captain, standing by with his own smoking pistol, refused to let anyone move the dying youth into the tent. The poor fellow lived for some days, but the captain continued to refuse to allow him to be taken into any shelter during that time. This final act of brutality damned the leader for ever in the eyes of his companions, and, though of necessity they had to live with him and share his subsequent adventures, the manner of Cozens' death was never forgotten.

The longboat was now examined for its seaworthiness, and it was decided to cut it in half and lengthen it by inserting a twelve-foot section amidships. From now on the hardiest men were put to work, under the direction of the carpenter, shaping timber and unpicking cable for oakum. While this work was going on the Indians returned, accompanied by their wives and families, to the number of fifty. Setting up their little shelters, they showed signs of having come to stay. Though friendly, it seemed as though they would be more of a liability than an asset, for they were wretchedly poor, and lived little better than their own dogs. They might have stayed with the whites, sharing their hardships, but for the fact that the disorderly sailors got out of control and attempted to seduce the Indian women, on discovering which the natives were so offended that they abruptly pulled up stakes and departed.

As the enlarging of the longboat progressed plans for escape to civilization were discussed. The majority were for the wild scheme of putting to sea and making their way home through the Straits of Magellan. But the captain's decision still had weight among the law-abiding ones, and the majority bowed to his veto of this plan. His own proposal was that they should make their way northward, seize a Spanish ship, and in it join Anson, who would probably be at the rendezvous, Juan Fernandez. Neither of these schemes came to anything, however. Meanwhile the spectre of starvation grew daily more menacing. The original number of men ashore, at one time about 145, had now dwindled to 100, and many were sick unto death. Byron was informed that he must sacrifice the Indian dog he had befriended. He pleaded for its life, but in vain; the men had for some time regarded it with hungry eyes. Byron himself, no less starved than the rest, was glad to accept a share of the flesh of his dead pet when its death had become a fact. Some idea of the famished condition of the men may be got from the statement of Byron's journal that, three weeks after the eating of the dog, its rotting skin and paws were dug up and eaten! And we will complain at a speck of dust in our teacup! One of the men would be absent for days hunting for food, his sole occupation being the stalking of birds, alone, like a solitary prowling wild animal. An occasional bird was shot near the camp. The birds are described as woodcock, sea fowl, birds of prey, and geese.

When work on the longboat was nearly finished Lieutenant Byron and thirteen men set out in the barge to explore the coast, a sort of preliminary reconnoitre. Such was their hunger that, when a few leagues to the south of Wager Island a bitch with a litter of puppies was found, the men had no hesitation in killing and eating them. The voyage was not a success, and after a few days they returned to Wager Island. They had visited a number of other islands, and one night, while sleeping ashore, had been frightened by a prowling wild beast. The weather had been consistently bad, making it too dangerous to keep at sea in an open boat in their weakened state, and even more dangerous to hug the uncharted, rockbound coast. Back at the camp they found hanging up, like clothes on a line, the quarters of slaughtered dogs. These had been brought by the Indians, who, for reasons best known to themselves, had decided to return to see the treacherous white men. They had come in six canoes, but prudently left their wives at home.

More momentous events than dogs' meat and Indian visits were afoot, however. The mutinous element had grown in numbers, and constituted a source of unending anxiety to the officers' party. The rebels were insisting that they should take the longboat and sail for England, taking Captain Cheap with them to stand trial for murder, murder of the young midshipman Mr Cozens. Those who doubted the men's seriousness no longer doubted when the longboat was launched and manned by the mutineers, who, bent on doing the thing in proper style, drew up a guard to arrest the captain. How this unpopular officer conducted himself during this time we do not know, but doubtless he remained cool. A sense of superiority, tinctured with a touch of insolence, goes a long way toward keeping a threatened man cool. However, Captain Cheap was not to suffer the ignominy of arrest by his own seamen, for on the persuasions of the minority party the rebels desisted from their intent, and with surly reluctance agreed that he should come as a passenger, not as leader. But the outraged captain announced that he preferred to remain behind.

Besides the longboat were two smaller boats, the larger craft carrying fifty-nine men, with twenty-two others divided between the two small boats, making a total of eighty-one men. Byron, who throughout seems to have remained loyal to Captain Cheap, was already in the longboat when he heard that the captain and a few others were remaining behind, and would have immediately gone ashore had this been possible, but his boat was then too far out. He wrote in his narrative:

> I was determined at the first opportunity to leave them, which at that instant was impossible for me to do, the longboat lying some distance off-shore, at anchor.

It was the intention of the men to work toward the mainland, putting into some cove or inlet every evening for prudence' sake. But bad weather was met with as soon as they left Wager Island, and the next day it was decided to send he barge back for some spare canvas to replace split and lost sails. Here young Byron saw his opportunity, and on some pretext got transferred to the returning boat. He now found, to his great satisfaction, that the men in the boat were already disheartened by the bad weather—their craft being so much smaller than the longboat—and were eager to return to Wager Island. Arriving there, they found Captain Cheap ready, for once, to be agreeable. But the position of the entire party was extremely serious. The boats' crews had taken most of the stores which had been salved from the wreck, and the men now gathered together

on the island had, for an indefinite stay, six pieces of pork, a like quantity of salt beef, and ninety pounds of flour. As this food had to be husbanded rigorously, the men eked out their pitiful ration with shreds of wild celery and rockweed fried in candle tallow. One is not surprised that Byron mentions having dysentery, and how some of the men were so weak they could scarcely drag one foot after the other. Surrounded by more or less loyal men, Captain Cheap resumed command of the depleted company, and sent a message to a small party of deserters camped across the bay to join his party. This they agreed to do, and came over in their boat. There were now in camp twenty men, with two leaky and rotten boats, their only means of escape from their island gaol. The carpenter had gone with the others, and there was no one among them with either the knowledge or the tools to repair the boats. The spirits of the party grew daily more gloomy. With the food nearly gone, it was a shock to discover that three of the men had sunk to thieving from the small supply left. One of the culprits escaped; the other two were caught, and sentenced to be flogged and banished to another island. One escaped before the sentence could be carried out, the other suffering the ordained penalty. Three days after the thief had been banished the compassionate Byron visited his isle in one of the boats, and on searching for the man found him dead. So Captain Cheap's unrelenting rule had found another victim.

About this time, when the entire party were so ill it seemed as though the end could not be far off, three casks of salt beef were delivered up by the wreck. The effect of this gift from the sea was immediately beneficial, and under its energizing effect Captain Cheap revived his plan of sailing northward — to Chilo, if possible — to capture a Spanish vessel and join Anson off the coast. It was such faith, such impudence, as this that made the English so feared on the west coast. These men, who could scarcely walk a hundred yards without falling, still had hopes of sailing in small open boats across stormy seas to the enemy's country, and, with a handful of cutlasses and a fowling-piece or two, of capturing one of their ships! Divine faith or egotistical impudence?

On December 15, midsummer in those parts, the little expedition set sail in the two small boats, and when well off the land encountered mountainous seas, which so endangered the boats that practically everything had to be thrown overboard to keep them afloat. Even the precious food had to be sacrificed. As nightfall approached the two boats were, with great risk, got ashore, and the men spent a terrible night wet, hungry, and without shelter. The next day a hunt for food brought them face to face with a number of seals, a most surprising and welcome sight. Before the unsuspecting creatures could escape a number of them lay dead, clubbed to death by the more active among the men.

The sea that had robbed them of their food now had made amends handsomely, and every one ate his fill of seal after an *hors-d'œuvre* of shellfish gathered among the rocks. But Fate had not yet finished sporting with the castaways. One of the boats, the yawl, capsized in the surf and swept out to sea after drowning one of the men. This loss of a boat made it impossible to proceed with the whole party, and four men, weary of the fight with the sea and willing to remain behind,

were left with arms and ammunition. They gave the barge three cheers as it pushed off, and were never heard of again, though later the barge, in charge of young Byron, was sent back to pick them up, but they could not be found. The narrative of their sufferings is too long for detailed telling here. Unspeakable hardships followed, until one marvels at the fortitude and temerity of the remaining men. Captain Cheap showed himself to be resolute and fearless, refusing at any time to acknowledge defeat, and by his example greatly heartening the rest. Byron, so young, a mere boy, had throughout shown exemplary courage and loyalty, and also the humanity that the captain lacked.

On one of the islands touched during this tragic odyssey the surgeon discovered what, at any other time, would have been of tremendous archæological interest. Entering a hole in a rock, he found himself in a long passage which led to a large chamber lighted from a shaft to the top. In this chamber stood a bier, a platform five feet high, on which lay six well-preserved and entirely naked Indian mummies. Near by was a second tomb.

The expedition, whose avowed purpose was to sail to Chilo and capture a Spanish vessel, was, after two months of fighting the elements, obliged to admit defeat. The

small boat was too deeply laden to continue in such seas, and the decision was reluctantly made to return to the scene of their earlier miseries, Wager Island.

> In three or four days after we arrived at our old station, Wager Island, but in such a miserable plight that, though we thought our condition upon setting out would not admit of any additional circumstance of misery, yet it was to be envied in comparison of what we now suffered, so worn and reduced were we by fatigue and hunger, having eaten nothing for some days but seaweed tangle.

So wrote Byron.

Back on Wager Island evidence of Indian visitors was at once noticed. Much of the gear that had been left behind was stolen. The little party of castaways was now reduced to eating pieces of leather, grass, and rotten scraps of meat washed up by the sea. Again, when it seemed that they must all surely perish, Fate granted them a further respite. A timely visit from a party of strange Indians revived hope. The chief spoke indifferent Spanish, but by this medium he was able to tell the white men how reports of the wreck had reached him through other tribes, and to explain that the badge he wore was bestowed upon him by the Spaniards, and indicated that he was the leading man of the tribe. Conversation was conducted with Captain Cheap through the surgeon, Mr Elliott, who knew a little Spanish. The chief was informed that the white men wished to reach a Spanish settlement, and would give him the barge and all its gear if he would conduct them thither. After some discussion the chief agreed to do this, and preparations were at once made for the journey. While it seemed to the men that their adventures were over, in reality they had only just begun.

The Indians led the Englishmen from one island to another, day after day, until it seemed as though there was no end to these islands. All this time the party was starving, and two men died in the boat, the second one to die begging for food up to the last. Lieutenant Byron afterward severely criticized Captain Cheap's conduct at this time, particularly his incredible selfishness. Though they had in the boat the remains of a seal that had been left by the Indians, the captain would not allow the dying man a morsel of this food, but took care that he himself had his full whack. Actually, by taking advantage of his rank, he fared better than the others, and in consequence his condition was better. And, though physically the strongest, he never would do his share of any labour or carry his part of a load.

Another blow was the stealing of the boat, in which were stored the arms and spare clothes, by six of the sailors, who made off in her. This, which at first looked to be a catastrophe of the first magnitude, was later acknowledged to be a good thing for the few left behind, for, as they afterward realized, the boat would have delayed their journey to civilization until they had all died. But for the moment they were marooned on one of the islands, and matters looked desperate, until they were rescued from the labyrinth of islands by a tribe of friendly Indians. After a journey of many days, during which they suffered so severely that Mr Elliott, the surgeon, died, and two others nearly succumbed, they were brought to the nearest Spanish settlement, where they were treated humanely despite the known purpose of their visit to Pacific waters. Captain Cheap, who had consistently ingratiated himself with the Indians, now behaved in a similar manner to his Spanish hosts, and appeared quite shameless where his own interests were concerned. His surname was a singularly appropriate one.

At the settlement the survivors ate like gluttons, and astonished their kindly hosts by their insatiable appetites. Conducted through the country, they at last came to the town of Castro, headquarters of the Governor. At one place, where they had stopped for a few days *en route*, the niece of the local priest, an attractive girl named Chloe, fell in love with Byron, but he reluctantly declined her favours, having no desire to settle in this wild land, the Protestant husband of a Spanish Catholic wife, spending the rest of his days among an alien people. Byron must have been something of an Adonis, for earlier he had been befriended and nursed by two young Indian women, who plainly had fallen in love with him.

From Castro they were taken to Santiago, Chile, where the commanding officer of the garrison generously offered to cash their drafts on the English consul at Lisbon, to the amount of 600 dollars, to enable them to purchase clothes and equipment. While nominally prisoners of war for two years, they were on parole, and mixed freely with local society, even making many friends among the Chileans. During their two years in Santiago they were housed, at his own expense, by a Scotch physician, Don Patricio Gedd,

who treated them like brothers. Eventually they were re-
leased, and put on a ship for France, from which country
they reached England, after an odyssey lasting nearly five
years. Of the eighty men who left Wager Island only thirty
survived. Apart from the captain's party, a few reached
England *via* Valparaiso. The six men who had made off in
the barge were never heard of again. So ends one of the
most prolonged and poignant experiences of hardship that
has ever been the fate of men to endure.

Some seventy-three years after the starving survivors of
the *Wager* had turned their backs on Patagonia for good the
crew and passengers of a French merchantman, the *Delphine*,
were cast on that inhospitable shore. The *Delphine*, under
Captain Coisy, left Le Havre for Valparaiso on March 30,
1814, with four passengers and a crew of sixteen. Rio was
reached within thirty days, and Staten Island was sighted
on May 30. Nine days later the Horn was rounded, and on
June 11, sailing through heavy seas and dangerous masses of
ice, Diego Island was seen. The bad weather, with much
fog, continued, and Captain Coisy was forced to navigate
more or less by guesswork. On the night of the 19th every
one on board was shaken by the *Delphine's* keel grinding on
submerged rocks, and now they found the ship literally
surrounded by rocks, some towering over the masts' trucks,
forbidding black crags. After recovering from the shock of
the collision all hands frantically set to work in an effort to
save the ship. But she was filling with water, and neither
pumping nor jettisoning the cargo would have been of any
use. At daybreak the launch was got over the side, and
rowed into a small bay. The ship had been wrecked on a
rocky island six miles long, and separated from the large
island of Campaña by a narrow channel. The captain and
a few men returned during the day to the wreck, which was
fast on the rocks half a mile from the beach, and came back
three hours later with the yawl, both boats bringing a mis-

cellaneous cargo. A temporary tent was erected, and a fire started, and the next two days were spent in eating, sleeping, and salvaging additional stores from the wreck. A few days later a sudden and violent squall partially wrecked the longboat by driving her on the rocks. The provisions secured from the wreck were calculated to last four months on short rations. As the winter season was beginning the castaways resigned themselves to wait for the spring before attempting to get away in the longboat, which, the carpenter decided, could be repaired.

There were ample signs that the island had been visited by savages: rude huts of tree branches, beneath which lay shells and the bones of animals. One night the captain's dog was heard to growl, and the next morning naked footprints were found near the camp—very Crusoe-ish this. Then, shortly afterward, one of the passengers, who had wandered from camp, returned excitedly to say that he had seen some Indians. The whites armed themselves and went out to meet the savages, who were practically naked and really harmless. The Indians wore nothing but a piece of sealskin, which hung down their backs. They were of middle height, strong, and well formed, but dirty, lazy, and dishonest. By their condition, their mode of life, and their brutish minds they seemed to have learned nothing from the whites during the seventy odd years since Lieutenant Byron had described them. They were always hungry, like the half-starved pack of dogs they kept for use in hunting seals.

By the month of September the carpenter had completed repairs to the longboat, which, in the process, had been decked and schooner-rigged, making her more fit to face a blue-water journey. Winter now being over, Captain Coisy decided to sail at once for San Carlos, on the island of Chilo, for assistance. At the first attempt to leave the water poured through the boat's rotten planking, and she had to be dragged ashore to be examined and recaulked. Though she again began to fill on the second launching, the captain insisted on sailing. With stores for eight days he departed, taking a Lieutenant Lepine and five men, which left thirteen men behind.

Now began a long period of waiting for those thirteen castaways, until their food was gone and they had given up hope. When the Indians gave them some dogs they showed their surprise at finding the dogs had been promptly eaten. The captain had departed on September 4, and it was not until the middle of November that he was able to return in a coasting vessel from San Carlos to pick up his companions. The boat's crew had had their own difficulties. It had taken them thirty-five days to reach San Carlos instead of a week, for they had been forced to land for shelter for days at a time owing to a succession of gales. And now the rescue vessel had come to pick up the men she had to stand off the land for three weeks before the sea would permit the launching of a boat.

Yet, in spite of this kind of thing, boys continued to run away to sea.

CHAPTER VI

The Lone Crusoe of Ruatan Island [1]

Then think of him,
Ye who rejoice, with those you love, at Eve,
When Winds of Winter shake the Window Frame,
And more endear your Fire—O think of him,
Who sav'd alone from the devasting Storm
Is cast on some deserted Rock, who sees
Sun after Sun descend, and hopeless hears
At Morn the long Surge of the troubled Main,
That beats without his wretched Cave; mean-time
He fears to wake the Echoes with his Voice,
So dread the Solitude!

W. L. Bowles, *The Spirit of Discovery*

IT gives the chronicler of these castaway tales not a little pleasure to include the narrative of a man who might be said to have outcrusoed Selkirk, if you'll allow the word. Our present hero, apart from his lonely exile, had one unique thing in common with Selkirk. Like the latter, his exile was self-imposed, and, if it was of lesser duration than the Scotsman's, he could at least boast (had he been so disposed) that his privations were proportionately greater, since he entered Crusoehood destitute of such provisions and gear as Selkirk would consider a *sine qua non*. But Philip Ashton, for that was his name, had taken the decision

---

[1] Also spelled Roatan. It lies about forty-five miles north of Honduras, and is thirty miles long by nine broad. Annexed by Great Britain in 1852, along with the smaller islands of the group to which Ruatan belongs, it was ceded to Honduras in 1859.

to become a Crusoe so precipitously that there had been no
time to collect the necessary stores, and his manner of overcoming this initial handicap is not the least interesting part
of his strange experience.

On Friday, June 15, 1722, an American trading schooner,
with a crew of four men and a boy, one of the men being
Philip Ashton, stood into Port Rossaway to lie there until
Monday. Arriving in the harbour, the schooner's crew
noticed an armed brig lying in the fairway, but thought
nothing of this until three or four hours later, when a boat
from the brig came across, and in a trice the schooner's
decks were in the possession of a group of armed men, who
demanded her surrender and that of the crew. Remon-
strances were in vain, and in broad daylight the schooner's
men were taken aboard the brig, where they found they had
been made prisoners by the notorious pirate Ned Low. This
worthy urged his prisoners to sign articles with him and
receive their share of anything taken, and hinted at rough
treatment to those who refused. The pirates had already
boarded other craft in the harbour and taken a number of
prisoners, who had been likewise invited to join the brig's
crew.

With five others Ashton was brought before Low, who
demanded to be told if any were married men. It was
a fair enough question, and, one would say, conveyed no
evil intent; but as the pirate spoke while flourishing a pistol
the prisoners remained mute—afraid to answer. Infuriated
at what he took to be defiance, Low put the pistol close
to Ashton's face, and shouted, "You dog, why don't you
answer me?" At this our man found his voice, replying,
with what courage he could muster, that he was not married.
If Ashton had been married the story of his Crusoe life would
never have been written, for it seemed that Low, having
recently lost his own wife, and having a child of his own
in Boston, would press no married men. Now Ashton,
as subsequent events show, must have been a man of an

unusually dogged character—ideal material from which to make a Christian martyr, for it was his persistent refusal to submit to the pirate's domination that led to his subsequent

sufferings. The pirates tried flattery and persuasion to recruit him, and as he continued to refuse to sign their articles they grew enraged, and told him he should serve them anyway. Henceforth his life became a dog's life. Putting to sea on June 19, the pirates left their slow-sailing brig to take possession of a faster schooner, while the brig, in which the unwanted prisoners were left, was ordered to stand for Boston. Ashton fell on his knees before Low, begging to be allowed to go in the brig, but the request was contemptuously refused. Ashton and seven other captives were kept to go aroving with the pirates.

Some time later, off St Michael's, they took a large Portuguese pink[1] laden with wheat, and as this vessel carried fourteen guns (which appear to have been of small use to her owners) the pirates transferred to her. A few days later, however, the prize sank while being careened, and the buccaneers had to return to the schooner, which had been kept with them. With the loss of the pink went most of the stores, and, being short of food, Low stood for Grenada, a French settlement, to obtain supplies. Here he kept most of his men hidden below, for such a crowd on that small vessel would have inevitably aroused suspicion. Philip Ashton, held among these rascals against his will, lived in daily fear of being caught by a man-of-war and hung as a pirate. This fear seems not to have been prompted so much by any cowardice, but by the thought of the disgrace that would be attached to his name.

After prowling about the gulf for some weeks and, having a variety of vicissitudes and adventures, the pirates again possessed two vessels instead of one. Captain Low had hoisted the Jolly Roger, and gone on board the prize, leaving his partner, a man with the curious name of Farrington Spriggs, in command of the schooner, with a division of the company, among whom was Ashton. The schooner's crew numbered twenty-two men, of whom eight were secretly plotting to capture the vessel and make off with her. Their plan was to take advantage of the fact that Spriggs had lost contact with Low during the last chase and to secure the pirates below hatches, after which they would put into the nearest port and give themselves up to the authorities. But Spriggs, having got wind of the plot, and falling in with Low

---

[1] A type of vessel now obsolete.

before it had been carried out, went on board the leader's vessel and told him of what was afoot. With the schooner covered by the guns of Low's vessel, Spriggs returned on board, resolved to punish the conspirators by shooting the four leaders, amongst whom he counted Philip Ashton. When taken before Spriggs, who was in an insane passion, Ashton, after listening to a fusillade of violent accusations, replied so moderately and with such reason that for the time being Spriggs's passion cooled, and the suspects escaped execution, though they were thereafter used with great harshness and severity, being selected for the most disagreeable work on board. But, whether or not this subdued the other malcontents, it certainly had the opposite effect on Ashton, who became more than ever resolved to escape at the first opportunity. Ever since the discovery of the plot he had been the special object of Spriggs's animosity, but, while he bore the ignominy in silence, deep within him he nursed an implacable resolve to get free of the hated slavery at the first opportunity, even if he should have to jump overboard. The chance came sooner than he expected.

On Saturday, March 9, 1723 (the date was an unforgettable one for our future Crusoe), when the schooner lay off Ruatan Island, the cooper was sent in the longboat with six men to go ashore for water. Ashton requested to be one of the boat party, but at first the cooper refused. Pressing the request, he urged that he had not once been off the ship, though the others had all had shore liberty. After some hesitation the cooper consented, and Ashton took an oar in the boat. In his narrative he tells us exactly what he wore when he left the schooner, a sartorial note we can appreciate the importance of in view of the experiment he was about to embark upon. Philip Ashton left his fellow-men and the comparative amenities of the schooner *with nothing in the world but an "Onasburgh frock and trousers, and a milled cap," and with neither shoes, stockings, nor anything else.* Despite this poverty of the commonest necessity, a knife, a pair of shoes, or flint and steel, he was determined never again to return to the schooner. But, as he was always suspect, the least false move would frustrate his plans, and bring on some brutal punishment, or possibly death. With a craftiness born of necessity, on landing he made a great business of filling the casks and rolling them to the water's edge, working as though his one thought was seeing the casks well and truly filled and put into the boat as expedi-

tiously as possible. Such solicitude for the schooner's water-supply, such devotion to duty, must surely disarm suspicion. When the barrels were filled the men lay about in the sun to rest awhile, but the indefatigable Philip, after taking a hearty draught of water, preferred to wander along the shore, picking up brightly coloured stones and shells. This sudden interest in shells aroused no suspicion, and he gradu-ally increased the distance between himself and the boat, until, when about the distance of a musket-shot, he began to edge toward the outskirts of the jungle, exulting that he had been allowed to wander so far without interference. Now his progress was halted by the cooper's gruff shout, demanding to know where he was going. Turning, he replied, " For coconuts," and pointed toward some coconut-palms on the fringe of the jungle. This appeared to satisfy the cooper, who allowed him to proceed. As casually as possible Ashton walked toward the nearest palms, frequently looking up as though his sole interest lay in coconuts. But once out of sight among the trees and tall undergrowth he ran as fast as his naked feet and the jungle thicket would allow. Such progress was necessarily slow, and after running for some time and getting well into the jungle he could still hear the voices of the men on the beach. Crouching under a dense thicket, he lay for what seemed an hour, listening, like a hunted animal. Presently the pirates began to call him, then he heard one say, " The dog is lost in the woods." To which another replied, "He has run away, and won't come out." For a while they continued to call, but Ashton had no intention of showing himself; and presently he heard the boat pushed off, and knew they had gone back to the schooner.

A sudden sense of loneliness swept over him at the boat's departure, though he never once wavered in his determination not to return to the pirates. He was alone and destitute, but he was free, and for the moment this was the only thing that mattered. Later, coming down to a small stream to drink, he saw the schooner still at anchor off-shore, but took care not to let himself be seen. Five days later, to his great joy, the pirates sailed away, leaving him to his solitude. During this time he had kept in hiding, only stealing out to gather fruit and to go to a stream for water. Now that he was in truth actually alone he began, like Selkirk and like Crusoe, to reflect upon his position. And when the full significance of it came to him he wept from the reaction of all he had been through, and the thought of how he had exchanged one evil for another. For what chance would a man have of survival on this uninhabited isle without weapons, tools, or the means of making a fire, apart from the matter of his sartorial deficiencies? So he felt now. Time alone would show. The only signs of other humans having been there before were fragments of Indian pottery, the sole reminders of a vanished race who once inhabited the island.

Fortunately there was no dearth of water, for, wandering among the hills, some of which rose to 900 feet, he came upon springs and cool streams hidden beneath the rich verdure in the deep valleys. Nor was there any lack of fruit, for figs, grapes, and coconuts could be had in abundance for the simple labour of picking them. On the hills were numbers of wild pigs, but he possessed neither the means of catching or cooking them. The idea occurred of digging pitfalls covered with light branches, but he lacked a shovel, and hands alone were insufficient to dig so deep. Even a fruit diet becomes a little monotonous after a time, and when one day, while poking in the sand, he uncovered four turtle eggs his delight was unbounded, and he ate them without inquiring too closely into their age. This success encouraged a further search, until he was presently rewarded by the discovery of a 'nest' containing no less than 150 eggs, which, happily, had not lain long enough to spoil. After eating his fill the rest were threaded like large beads on a strip of palmetto and hung in the sun to dry, a process which made them distinctly leathery, but not, he avowed, unpalatable.

If Ashton was without human companions he was not without companions of a less comforting kind. Of the wild pigs we have heard, but there were other creatures in the jungle of a less appetizing kind, for he speaks of "many serpents," large snakes, some fourteen feet long and "as large as a man's waist." These were of the boa species, and not poisonous, though, having no effective weapon against their dangerous coils, he gave them a wide berth. Sometimes, however, he would come upon them unawares stretched out along a tree branch, almost perfectly camouflaged by their form and protective colouring. The first

SOLITUDE

time he saw one he was almost upon it before discovering it was a snake, and then only by the creature opening its thin red jaws. Another creature, less affrightening but much more of a nuisance, was a small black fly, which attacked in armies and tormented the half-clothed man to distraction.

He had now been on the island several months, during which time he had not even seen a distant sail, though he would climb to a hill-top and sit for hours watching the horizon. And, though at times feeling the loneliness almost overpoweringly, he never regretted leaving the pirates. A deeply religious vein sustained him in this. Coming from Puritan New England, the manners and ethics of the pirates had profoundly shocked him, and any martyrdom, it seemed, would be preferable to enduring the swaggering, blasphemous ways of his captors. Still, as he sat on the hill-tops silently watching the sea he did not give up hope of ultimately being rescued.

And what of his condition, his way of living, his home, after months of being a Crusoe? Of meat, of course, he had none, unless we accept turtle eggs and an occasional meal of shellfish, but the fruit-supply was inexhaustible, and he thrived on it. His house, if it could be regarded as such, was what could be built with hands alone, unaided by tools. This, a primitive sort of hut of branches, thatched with leaves against the dew by night and the sun by day, stood near the coast, within view of the sea, whence his deliverers must come. The manner of building his home was simple.

Against a horizontally growing and low-hanging bough he leaned a number of stripped branches, secured by withes of split palm leaves. Afterward a number of others were constructed along the coast on the same principle, and all placed with their open sides facing the sea. Thus, when absent from his main dwelling and overtaken by night, he could sleep in one of these shelters.

Lying off the main island and divided from it by shallow channels were smaller isles, which Ashton would regard

longingly as places in which to escape from the maddening pest of flies. But, being an indifferent swimmer, he dared not venture swimming across. Having no tools, a canoe was out of the question, but the desire germinated another idea which offered no insuperable difficulties. This was the making of a small support of bamboo, a crude miniature raft, to which he could cling while swimming over to the nearest islet, which lay, as he would describe it, "at gunshot distance." This isle, or key, as it is called in the West Indies, was only three or four hundred yards round, and though without the verdure of its larger brother it was free from the pest of flies, and therefore a welcome refuge to the tormented man. Lying very low and clear of jungle, nothing impeded the winds of the sea from blowing across it. So our Crusoe made it a habit to retire to this spot during the middle of the day, when the heat made the insects intolerable. He preferred this barren key to the larger island, but, as it would have been impossible to live on this isle of refuge, he took great care to carry the little raft beyond the reach of the tide on landing there. Even so, these excursions were never free from dangers of one kind or another. Once the raft slipped from under him and he was swept away by the current, but, being near in, was able to fight his way to the beach. Fortunately he was on the 'homeward' journey. On another occasion a shovel-nose shark rushed at him, striking him on the thigh just as his feet touched bottom. The blow left a large bruise, but by extraordinary good fortune he was able to get ashore without worse happening. When swimming across he would carry his frock and trousers in a tight bundle secured on top of his head. By practice he became a better swimmer, and in course of time visited other keys within his range.

During most of his stay on Ruatan Ashton suffered agonies from his bare feet on broken shells, sticks and stones, and the hot sand. The deep cuts in the soles of his feet began to make long excursions about the island impossible. He would sit for hours staring out to sea, sometimes all day, too listless from the heat to desire food, and suffering too much with his lacerated feet to wander. Once, while feeling more than usual the tropical lassitude, a wild pig, unwarning, rushed out of the undergrowth, all tusks and concentrated fury. Having no strength to resist such an attack, he caught the lowest bough of the tree under which he had been sitting and swung, like a monkey, out of the way of the danger, but not without losing the seat of his trousers as the sharp tusks gave a wicked, upward thrust. Unlike a hungry wolf, the boar did not remain under the tree until its victim was forced to descend, but, without waiting, trotted off whence it had come. This was the only time Ashton was attacked by any wild creature during his stay on the island.

Further months passed, and his physical weakness increased until he scarcely had the strength to gather fruit. Only by an effort of will could he make himself pick grapes

and figs or search the shore for shellfish. He often craved a fire, and in vain tried to produce one by rubbing sticks together. The rainy season had come, bringing chill winds which penetrated his primitive shelter no matter what he did to prevent them. With physical degeneration came a mental decline, or, rather, a loss of the powers of concentration and memory. He lost all count of the days, which,

129

up till then, had been scrupulously kept. Lying shivering in the hut, his thoughts dwelt morbidly on death, until he longed for the end to quit this miserable existence. He thought much of home, and would become lachrymose. His deeply religious nature caused him to dwell on his past sins and pray for forgiveness from his Maker. From what we have seen of his conduct so far this repentance seems unnecessary, but he felt otherwise, and got much solace from calling himself a miserable sinner.

Some time toward the end of November—the date could only be guessed at—after being nearly nine months on the island, he descried out to sea a small speck, which grew larger until it became a canoe, and in the canoe was a man. According to all rules, our castaway should have been delirious with joy at the prospect of relief from the corroding loneliness. But Ashton had got beyond the state of feeling the normal reactions to such a momentous discovery. He was too ill to experience either pleasure or fear, and continued to sit where he had been sitting from the first, while the stranger approached the shore. He, on the other hand, showed some surprise and distrust at the unmoving man sitting on the beach staring toward him, showing no inclination to come and welcome him. The stranger called out, distrustful of the sitting man's mysterious immobility. Understanding the other's hesitation, Ashton shouted out that there was nothing to fear, he could safely come ashore, and further indicating by words and gestures that he, Ashton, was too weak from illness to do anyone harm. The stranger turned out to be an old Indian "of venerable aspect and reserved temper." He had lived twenty-two years with the Spaniards, but had recently been forced to flee from them for some trouble. He had in the canoe a gun, with powder and shot, and a small quantity of pork. He announced his desire and intention of spending the rest of his days on the island, supporting himself by hunting. His first action was to share the pork with the white man, a generous and friendly gesture that warmed the lonely cast-away to his dusky visitor. The Indian, after these pre-liminary introductions, sat silent for a long time, and proved thereafter to be of that taciturn disposition which is so characteristic of the Indian race. For two days he remained with Ashton, sharing the scrap of pork and foraging for fruit. On the third day he announced his intention of paddling over to a neighbouring island for wild hogs and deer, and invited Ashton to accompany him. But, though willing to do so, the latter was so crippled by his lacerated and swollen feet that a hunting trip was beyond his powers; and so the Indian, with promises to return with fresh meat, departed alone. He had come from North Britain Island, a distance of twelve leagues from Ruatan, and the little voyage to one of the neighbouring islands would involve no hazards at all for such a man. On this morning the sea and sky were serene; there was no thought of danger, and Ashton greatly regretted his inability to accompany the Indian. But within an hour of his leaving clouds hid the sun, and a violent squall churned those waters into a seething cauldron within a few minutes. Ashton at once feared for the safety of his friend, and, as he never returned, it was reasonably certain that he had perished. So, after this brief interlude of com-pany for three days, Ashton found himself once more alone. But he was now considerably better off, for he had, besides five pounds of pork, a bottle of gunpowder, tobacco, a knife, and a piece of flint. This latter treasure was the most precious of all, for it meant a fire, an inestimable comfort in the rainy season. With a change of diet, dressed meat (roast pork, turtle, and crayfish), his strength noticeably improved, though his feet remained a source of trouble, keeping him more or less crippled. The method of catch-ing crayfish was original. With a bundle of broken sticks, which burned like pitch-pine, he would wade in the shallows in the night, using the sticks as a torch, while the crayfish, attracted by the light, would crawl round his feet. With a forked twig, it was an easy matter to toss the dazzled crustaceans ashore, where he would broil them over a fire.

Two or three months after losing his companion he came upon a small canoe on the shore, empty and quite seaworthy. At first it appeared as if it might be the lost Indian's canoe, but on examination it proved not to be, a discovery that set Ashton wondering if some unwelcome visitors might be in the neighbourhood.

But as no human creatures appeared to claim it, his qualms subsided, and he began to use the little craft to make excursions to his former isle of refuge. The success of this mode of transport gave him the idea of venturing farther afield, and he decided to visit two larger and more distant islands standing out of the sea, dim silhouettes in blue. Stocking the canoe with figs, grapes, and a small tortoise, and taking the precious flint, he set out for an island[1] five or six leagues, he judged, from Ruatan. When well off the land he sighted a schooner to the eastward, and so altered his course to the west for fear the strange vessel might be a pirate. The buccaneers favoured small, fast schooners, and all schooners in the Caribbean and the Gulf of Mexico were suspect until they had proved otherwise. And Ashton remained in mortal fear of pirates. He would, he reiterated, rather die than again live with those hated men.

But he reached Bonacca Island apparently unseen, and

[1] This was Bonacca Island.

hauled the canoe up beyond high-water mark. His feet still
gave him much trouble, and it took him two days to make
his way (mostly by crawling on hands and knees) across a
point of land where he could watch the schooner. So great
was his fear of being taken by pirates that he went through
all this agony to avoid being surprised by them, and this
without any proof that the schooner was a pirate. Crawling through the woods, he came at last to the place where

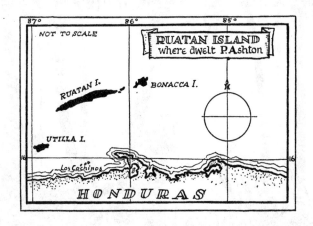

he judged the schooner would be lying, and cautiously
approached the coast, being careful to keep within the cover
of the woods. But on debouching opposite the coast he
found the schooner nowhere in sight. Thoroughly exhausted, he lay down, and slept until he was abruptly
awakened by the sound of musket-fire. Feeling safe, he had
lain exposed to view from the sea, and he now beheld the
astonishing sight of a number of canoes crowded with
Spaniards, who were actually firing at him. A curious piece
of psychology this, that prompted them to shoot at a sleeping
man without ascertaining anything about the unfortunate
creature : a motive due probably to some form of hysteria. At
any rate, Ashton, without troubling to analyse the Spaniards'
motives, took to his poor heels and disappeared into the

133

labyrinth of the jungle. As he ran the bullets ripped through the twigs on either side of him, and he heard his pursuers shouting, "O Englishman! we will give you good quarter." Having small reason to trust them, he kept on running until he got deep into the jungle, where he lay

hiding for several hours until he heard them departing. Cautiously reconnoitring, he came to the spot where he had been surprised, and saw the schooner sailing away. As she flew English colours, he concluded that she had been captured by the Spaniards in the Bay of Honduras. Embedded in the bole of the tree that he had been sleeping against were no less than six bullets!

It took him three days to cross to the beach where he had left the canoe, and he was overjoyed to find it still there. The island had no such abundance of fruit as Ruatan, and during the six days there he nearly starved, so that, what with the pest of insects of all kinds, he was glad to return to Ruatan, which he safely reached at nightfall.

The long periods of Philip Ashton's complete isolation would be as devoid of interest to the reader as they were to him. After the alarming experience on Bonacca Island he spent another seven months alone, hunting for food and ranging the island when his feet would permit. At this time he seems to have got a sort of spiritual second wind, inasmuch as we no longer hear of repinings and despair. Experience with white men had not fed his desire to return to them, and he was slowly coming to accept a situation that would have crushed less resolute men. Then, about the month of June 1724, while on the isle of refuge, he saw two canoes full of white men approaching. They had seen the smoke from his camp-fire, but now held off, watching, as uncertain of Ashton as he was of them. They knew not how many others might be hiding within the bushes. Taking advantage of the fact that his canoe lay out of sight beyond a point of the coast, Ashton quietly slipped away and made for Ruatan. The men in the canoes saw him paddle over, and approached cautiously. Ashton retreated within the shelter of the trees, determined not again to expose himself to bullets. Calling to them, he asked who they were. They drew nearer, and asked if he was alone. Finding that they were Englishmen, he decided to trust them, and informed them that he was an Englishman escaped from pirates. These men seemed to have been extraordinarily cautious, for on landing they drew back at the approach of the ragged Crusoe. But compassion mastered their aversion, and Ashton found himself embracing the first man to come up to him. The visitors gently carried him to one of their boats, where he was asked to relate his story, every one being astonished at this ragged, hairy man they had found. He told them how, save for the three days with the Indian, he had been alone for sixteen months, and how he had begun his solitary life without food or weapons or means of making fire, and only half-clad. They stood amazed at his recital, and, seeing him exhausted at the end of the tale, gave him a spoonful of rum; but its effect on his weakened body was so potent that he fell insensible, which caused his rescuers much anxiety until he recovered.

The party, led by two men, John Hope, an old man whom they called Father Hope, and John Ford, were eighteen in number, all belonging to the Bay of Honduras, whence they had fled from the Spaniards. The two leaders had already been among these islands,[1] and knew them well. And now, being dispossessed by the Spaniards, they had come in two boats, with an Indian woman to cook for them, to begin life again as settlers on the islands. They had brought a limited quantity of provisions, mainly flour, and a dog for hunting, together with firearms and fish-nets.

On Barbarat Island, two leagues from Ruatan, Hope and Ford had had in former days a plantation, on which they now proposed to settle. Near Barbarat lay an islet about 450 yards in circumference, and named by them 'Castle of Comfort' on account of the absence of trees, thus leaving it open to breezes from the sea, a most effectual preventive against visiting mosquitoes. They took Ashton to their hearts, treating him with rough kindliness and making him one of themselves. After nursing him back to health our Crusoe might be suspected of being a prig when he wrote, "Yet, after all, they were bad society; and as to their common conversation, there was little difference between them and pirates." But as his rigid creed saw no evidence of any present dishonesty, "as rendered it unlawful to join them, or be found in their company," he continued to live among them, though, as we suspect, keeping certain mental reservations to himself. Here we hang on to his narrative, praying, almost, that he won't disappoint us by turning ingrate and moralizing at the expense of his benefactors,

---

[1] They are known as the Bay Islands.

even while accepting their bread. So, keeping his thoughts to himself, he lived among them, hunting wild hog and deer, after his strength returned. They would visit different islands for game, sometimes going no farther than the shore, where the huge sea-turtles were to be found. The slaughtered deer or hogs would be brought back to their home camp, where the flesh would be dried and smoked in the *boucans*, from which, as we have seen, the buccaneers got their name. After half a year of this life three of them, with Ashton, took a four-oared canoe to hunt on Bonacca Island, while the others arranged to return to Honduras to fetch the remaining possessions, if it were unsafe for them to return there for good. Owing, however, to various circumstances, their departure for the main was delayed, and meanwhile Ashton and his three companions were on their way home with the canoe loaded with wild hogs and a few turtles. As they paddled toward the little bay in the moonlight they saw a flash followed by the report of a gun which came from a large *periagua*[1] lying off the Castle of Comfort. This report was followed by the rattle of musket-fire, and the four hunters realized that some one was attacking their people. The four men waited no longer, but turned to escape, were pursued, and nearly caught by the unknown enemy, who had seen them in the moonlight. They were chased to an island a mile and a half distant by an eight-oared boat of some kind, which carried a swivel that discharged shot uncomfortably close.

A touch of unconscious humour entered the drama when the pursuers called out that they were pirates and not Spaniards, as though that made all the difference. And Ashton says:

> Yet nothing could have been said to discourage me more from putting myself in their power. I had the utmost dread of pirates; and my original aversion was enhanced by the apprehension of being sacrificed for my former diversion.

[1] Canoe.

But the four men escaped into the woods, being forced to leave their canoe on the beach, where the pirates took possession of it. It is interesting to note that Ashton did not regard this as so much of a calamity as did his companions, who, unlike him, had not served an apprenticeship in destitution. The loss of the canoe hardly troubled our Crusoe at all, he was so profoundly thankful to have escaped the pirates. And, as he pointed out, they still had their firearms and flint. What else could man desire?

Their assailants, they afterward found out, were men belonging to Farrington Spriggs, Ashton's particular enemy, who had left Captain Low and set up in business on his own account. He possessed a twenty-four-gun ship and a sloop of twelve guns, obtained in the usual way, no doubt. Both vessels were then lying in the harbour at Ruatan, opposite the same spot where Ashton had run away from them long before. As on the former occasion, the pirates had come in to fill their water-casks. They captured the other men—who, to their sorrow, had been delayed in their departure for the main—and abused them cruelly for several days before setting them afloat in a small craft without provisions.

Truly the way for pioneers was hard in the Americas two hundred years ago. The two old men, Hope and Ford, after a lifetime of vicissitude and struggle to live, found themselves robbed of everything and set adrift in a small boat with small hope of surviving such an ordeal. Philip Ashton learned that the pirates would have killed him if he had been taken, intelligence which made him more than ever on the alert against his dreaded enemies.

When Spriggs' two vessels had departed Ashton and his three companions, who had been hiding in the jungle, were surprised to see the small boat in which the captives had been set adrift, now appear, and presently Hope and Ford came ashore. The men had craftily hung about in the offing until the pirates had departed, and now offered to take off their friends and stand for the Bay of Honduras.

Still in mortal fear of the pirates, Ashton declined the invitation, though two of his companions departed in the boat. He was now left with one of the men[1] and a newcomer, a negro slave who elected to stay ashore. They were also left two dogs, a canoe, and firearms. For two or three months the trio ranged the islands, hunting in order to live. The dreaded rainy season was approaching, and Ashton had resigned himself to another 'winter' on Ruatan

when a brigantine from Salem, Massachusetts, commanded by a Captain Dove, put in for water, and so was the means of his deliverance, and that of his two companions. Our Crusoe reached Salem on May 1, 1725—two years and nearly two months after landing on the island of Ruatan, a name he probably never wanted to hear again as long as he lived.

Philip Ashton's experience is another reminder that truth is stranger than fiction. Except on the score of time, he outdid Selkirk, inasmuch as he began with nothing, not even so much as a knife. Actually, this seemingly frightful handicap is not so serious to a strong and resourceful man. As I will show in a moment, it is possible for a man to begin with literally nothing, not even clothes, and succeed in

[1] John Symonds.

keeping himself alive indefinitely. It is not the material obstacles that count for so much in these Crusoe records as the mental, the psychological ones—the dreadful loneliness. It is this, and nothing more, that puts Robinson Crusoe among the fiction list. It is the incredible span of years spent alone that is beyond the range of possibility. Selkirk's four years and a bit would take some believing were it not that it is verified by unimpeachable witnesses. Coming back to the merely physical side of these tales, I would like to refer briefly to the interesting experiment of Joseph Knowles, a man of forty-four, who, on August 4, 1913, in the presence of a number of witnesses, including newspaper reporters, went into the Maine woods stark naked to prove his contention that man could live in the primitive woods without clothing and with nothing but his hands to aid him. And two months later he emerged dressed in skin clothing which he had made himself from wild animals he had caught. During those two months he never spoke to a human being nor received any outside aid whatsoever. And the irony of it all was that, after he had carried out this really remarkable experiment, he was summoned by the State authorities for killing game without a permit and fined $205.

He was burnt brown like an Indian. His hair and beard had grown long and matted, and his bare arms were covered with a multitude of scratches from the underbrush of the northern Maine woods, which, incidentally, are as much a wilderness now as when the Pilgrim Fathers landed on Plymouth Rock. He wore a sort of sleeveless coat made from the skin of a black bear, secured in front with deer thongs. On his legs were roughly fashioned chaps of deer-skin. On his feet were moccasins of buckskin sewn with deer sinew. A hat he had none, nor needed one, for the sun is not hot in those latitudes. As for rain, it was raining the afternoon he started out naked. This did not greatly bother him. Over his shoulders hung a crude sack made by plaiting the inner bark of the cedar. From his waist hung a piece of deer-horn used for a knife, and he carried in one hand a bow and arrows.

Locally his feat created extraordinary excitement and interest, and in view of its uniqueness it is curious that the experiment did not become more widely known. It is only fair to say that this disciple of Thoreau had lived an outdoor life, and knew a great deal about woodcraft. A townsman could not have succeeded in such a rigorous experiment. How he caught wild animals, slept, ate, dressed, and generally existed was told fully in contemporary newspapers, and afterward published in book form.

CHAPTER VII

The Narrative of Captain Flinders' Crusoes

Alarming Thought! for now no more a-lee
Her trembling side could bear the invading sea,
And if pursuing waves she scuds before,
Headlong she runs upon the frightful shore.

WILLIAM FALCONER, *The Shipwreck*

IN September 1803 the Governor of New South Wales received from Captain Matthew Flinders, of the Royal Navy, a letter acquainting him of the loss of two ships and the casting away of their crews on a coral reef. The first news of the disaster reached the public through an announcement in the *Sidney Gazette* at Port Jackson, of which the following is a copy:

> Captain Flinders, late Commander of H.M. Sloop *Investigator*, and Mr Park, Commander of the Ship *Cato*, arrived at Government House, at half-past three in the afternoon of the eighth Instant [September 1803], with the following disagreeable intelligence, as communicated in a letter to his Excellency:[1]

> SIDNEY, NEW SOUTH WALES
> *September* 9, 1803
> SIR,
> I have to inform you of my arrival here yesterday, in a six-oared Cutter, belonging to his Majesty's armed Vessel *Porpoise*, commanded by Lieutenant Fowler, which Ship, I am sorry to state to your Excellency, I left on shore upon a Coral Reef, without any prospect of her being saved, in latitude 22° 11′ South, and longitude

---

[1] Governor Philip Gidley King, Post-Captain R.N.

155° 13′ East: being 196 miles to the N., 38° East from *Sandy Cape*, and 729 miles from this Port. The Ship *Cato*, which was in Company, is entirely lost upon the same Reef, and broken to pieces, without anything having been saved from her: but the Crew, with the exception of three, are, with the whole of the Officers, Crew, and Passengers of the *Porpoise*, upon a small Sand Bank, near the Wrecks; with sufficient Provisions, and Water saved from the *Porpoise*, to subsist the whole, amounting to 80 Men, for three months.

Accompanied by the Commander of the *Cato*, Mr John Park, and twelve Men, I left Wreck Reef in the Cutter, with three weeks Provisions, on Friday, *August* the 26th, in the Morning; and on the 28th, in the Evening, made Land near *Indian Head*, from whence I kept the coast on board to this place.

I cannot state the extent of Wreck Reef to the Eastward, but a Bank is visible in that direction, six or seven Miles from the Wrecks. In a West direction we rowed along the Reef twelve Miles; but saw no other dangers in the passage towards *Sandy Cape*. There are several passages through the Reef, and Anchorage in from 15 to 22 fathoms, upon a sandy Bottom: the Flag-staff bearing S.E. to S.S.W. distance from three quarters to one and a quarter mile.

After the above Statement it is unnecessary for me to make Application to your Excellency, to furnish me with the means of relieving the Crews of the two Ships from the precarious situation in which they are placed: since your Humanity, and former unremitting attention to the *Investigator* and *Porpoise*, are sureties, that the earliest and most effectual means will be taken; either to bring them back to this Port, or to send them, and myself, onward towards England.

I have the honour to be

Your Excellency's

Obedient humble Servant,

MATTHEW FLINDERS

The *Porpoise*, in company with the East India Company's extra ship *Bridgewater* and the ship *Cato*, on August 17, 1803, at two o'clock in the morning, fell in with an uncharted sandbank 196 miles east from Sandy Cape, on the coast of

New South Wales. The disaster, like so many of the kind in those pioneer days, was due solely to imperfect charting. The signal had been made to keep under easy sail during the night, the *Porpoise* being in the van, with the *Cato* and *Bridgewater* on the port and starboard quarters respectively. A warrant officer was stationed as look-out on the *Porpoise*,

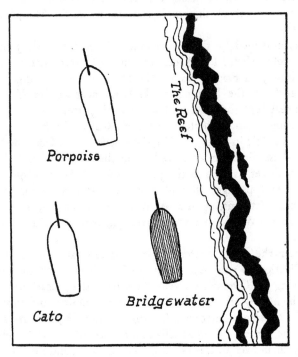

which was sailing on a course N.N.W., with a faint breeze from E.S.E. At 8 p.m. a sounding gave thirty-five fathoms with no bottom. At 9.30 breakers were seen directly ahead, and the helm was put hard down, but while paying off the keel struck a coral reef, and the ship was instantly in a pandemonium of confused noises of the breaking seas and shouted commands. An attempt was made to warn her consorts astern by firing a gun, but, owing to the heavy seas breaking over the labouring vessel, the attempt was rendered impossible. While signal rockets were being fetched the two ships astern had hauled to wind across each other on different tacks. In the darkness and confusion it was not quite clear how it happened, but the only important thing was that the two vessels must have collided and gone on the reef together had not the commander of the *Cato*, with great presence of mind, instantly stopped setting the main-sail, and, instead, bore away to let the *Bridgewater* pass to windward, and thus clear the breakers. The fortunate ship stood away to the south, where for the nonce we will leave her.

But now, in the language of the sea, the *Cato* missed stays, and crashed on to the reef two cables' length from the unlucky *Porpoise*. Thus, within the space of a few minutes, two noble ships were piled up on the reef. The *Porpoise* lay over on her bilge toward the shore, in which position the seas broke over without filling her. In order to ease her the main- and mizen-masts were cut. The fore-mast had already gone by the board. The *Cato*, on the other hand, took the opposite inclination, so that the seas filled her immediately, and drove the crew into the lee fore-chains, where, constantly drenched and perished with cold, they remained all night, expecting every minute to be their last. An hour after the *Porpoise* had struck, two boats, the gig and a six-oared cutter, were launched to leeward, but the cutter was almost immediately stove against the ship. Captain Flinders had observed that the breakers did not extend far to leeward, and, suspecting the significance of this, informed Lieutenant Towler of his intention of getting the charts of this coast made by the *Investigator*,[1] and going in the gig on board the *Bridgewater* to obtain assistance. With six of the best oarsmen, the gig was got through the surf safely, though nearly full, and floated in smooth water over a coral reef just below the keel. As the *Bridgewater* was drawing

---

[1] The *Investigator* had been on a survey, charting the south-west coast of New Holland some time before.

farther away in the darkness the attempt to reach her was abandoned, and Flinders returned to the wreck, but, as the surf was running too high to attempt boarding, the boat was rowed gently in the lee of the breakers till daylight. They could see the cutter, temporarily repaired, riding to her painter. Those on board the *Porpoise* burned a number of blue lights during the night, which appeared to be answered by a winking light from the *Bridgewater*, which did not,

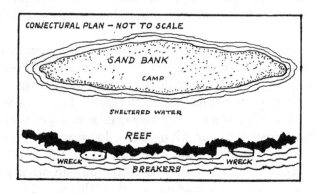

however, approach closer. At daybreak Flinders boarded the *Porpoise* by using one of the fallen masts as a bridge.

In full daylight a low sandbank could be seen a few cables' length to leeward, and, as temporary refuge, appeared large enough to hold the companies of both vessels. The shipwrecked men were further heartened by the sight of the *Bridgewater*, which, though some miles away, appeared to be standing down to them. Every one on board the *Porpoise* was set to work getting stores and water into the boats and on a raft that had been hastily put together. While the stores and water-casks were being ferried across to the bank Captain Flinders made another effort to reach the *Bridgewater*, his purpose being to indicate to her commander the sheltered anchorage where the shipwrecked crews could be taken on board. But, to the disappointment of every one and the curses of many, the

Bridgewater stood away, and slowly disappeared below the horizon.

As the tide fell the *Cato's* people were able to leave her, and wade through the surf to the *Porpoise's* small boat, which carried them to the sandbank. Afterward, when the whole company had assembled on the bank, Captain Flinders came up to the fire built by the men of the *Porpoise* for the *Cato's* crew, who were cold and terribly bruised by swimming through the surf, and asked Mr Mart, the carpenter, where he had procured his firewood. The carpenter told him that it was part of the stern-post of an ancient wreck found buried in the sand. They thought that it might be part of one of La Pérouse's lost frigates,[1] though in this surmise they were mistaken, for the two frigates were wrecked on the island of Vanikoro, in the New Hebrides, and the most baffling sea mystery of the century was not solved until over twenty years after Captain Flinders had seen the pieces of the old stern-post on the sandbank.

At low water the nearly dry reef was used as an unloading lighter, from which the provisions, water, and other stores were taken across to the sandbank in the boats. Before nightfall five hogsheads of water, flour, meat, rice, salt, spirits, and several pigs and sheep had been safely got across to the bank. As the *Cato's* people had left their ship in varying degrees of nudity, Lieutenant Fowler, of the *Porpoise*, found them some officers' uniforms, which, to their amusement and confusion, they put on. That night the entire company, wrapped in blankets and great-coats, slept on the sand round the fire, save for the watch. The three boats were hauled up at night under the lee of the bank, but the small boat, not so well secured, broke loose the first night and was carried off by the tide. Here was a large company wrecked on a sandbank very similar to the Cargados Garayos bank on which the men of the *Cabalva* were wrecked in 1818, but here the resemblance ends, for the

[1] See *Ships and Sailors* by the present author.

present company were mostly naval men, used to naval discipline, and commanded by efficient officers, who were not of the temper to tolerate such a comic-opera mutiny as happened on the Cargados Garayos.

Though Captain Flinders was the senior officer, he had been travelling in the *Porpoise* as a passenger, being on his way to Sydney from duty elsewhere. But when it became plain that the *Porpoise* could not be saved he took command. His first act was to divide the *Cato's* people, who had saved nothing, among the men of the *Porpoise*, quartering them in messes in the proportion of one in three. Lieutenant Fowler was sent off to the *Porpoise*, in charge of salvage parties, with the two cutters, to bring off anything useful, especially provisions. The *Cato's* usefulness could be ruled out, as that ill-fated craft had broken up during the night.

During the next two days the wind blew fresh from the south-east, and as the *Bridgewater* did not return it was supposed that her commander, Captain Palmer, was beating to windward, waiting for fine weather before returning to pick up the castaways. But when on the 21st and 22nd—the days being fine—he did not appear the marooned men gave up hope of assistance from that quarter. During these four days they had worked every possible moment on the wreck, bringing off stores, water, sails, and cordage. Captain Flinders gathered round him his principal officers to discuss what steps to take now that there was no hope of the *Bridgewater* returning. The plan which received most favour was, firstly, to have the large cutter lightly decked over and have her proceed, with Captain Flinders and Mr Park, commander of the *Cato*, with a picked crew, to Port Jackson for assistance; secondly, in case of the loss of the first boat a smaller boat should be built from wreckage by the carpenter, and proceed, after two months, to Port Jackson in charge of a competent officer.

By the evening of August 23 nearly the whole of the

provisions and water of the *Porpoise* had been carried over to the sandbank. It might interest some readers to see the purser's tabulated list of stores, with the number of days they would last the ninety-four men at full allowance.

Biscuits 920 lb.	} 83 days	Spirits	225 gallons	} 49 days
Flour 6944 „		Wine	113 „	
Beef 7104 „	} 94 „	Porter	60 „	
Pork 1184 „		Water	5650 „	
Pease 45 bushels 107 .,		at ¼ gallon per day 120 „	
Oatmeal 30 „ 48 „			
Rice 1225 „ 114 „		Also miscellaneous stores—
Sugar 370 lb.	} 84 „	sourkrout, essence of malt, salt,
Molasses 125 „		and vinegar, etc.

A most comforting list we should say, especially when comparing it with the fare of the men on Boon Island, or Richard Falconer on the Alcrane Reef. It would, however, have gone hard with these ninety odd men had nothing been salved, for they were on a sand-bank barren of anything either edible or potable. Besides the great quantity  of food stores, sails, spars, cordage, iron-work, an anchor, a forge, arms and ammunition were also brought ashore. While the salvage parties were getting the stores out of the wreck the carpenter, with a number of helpers, was preparing the cutter, which was christened *Hope*, for the long journey to the mainland. On Thursday, August 25, the boat was ready, and the next morning, nine days after being wrecked, Captain Flinders, with thirteen men and three weeks' provisions, embarked on the journey for assist-ance. As the boat put off three cheers came from eighty throats, and the reversed ensign was hauled down and hoisted again with the union in the upper canton.

On the bank Lieutenant Fowler was left in command, with Lieutenant Flinders (the captain's brother) under him. Fowler, like all good officers, kept a log, and we are allowed to peep into it. Beginning on August 19, the day after the people came on to the bank, he tells how busy they were that day bringing off stores from the *Porpoise*, and how, by dusk, they had landed three tons of fresh water, six hogsheads each of peas and flour, one each of spirits, wine, and pork, two each of rice and oatmeal, one tierce of beef, half a hogshead of sugar, eight sheep, eight hogs, and a number of fowls. A good day's work! The ship had lifted farther on the reef, thus lightening the work of salvage. The sandbank lay very low, and Lieutenant Fowler expresses the opinion that in bad weather it would be untenable, as it would be overswept by the sea.

On the second day tents were erected, and a topsail yard stood up and stayed for a flagstaff. On the 23rd the flagstaff was the scene of a flogging, one of the seamen receiving a dozen lashes for drunkenness on board the wreck. To prevent pilfering a sentinel was posted night and day over each food dump. Despite this precaution, on the 28th a seaman contrived to steal some lime-juice, but, being caught, was awarded twenty-eight lashes of the cat. After the *Hope* had gone Fowler put every one on rations, but generous enough to give no cause for complaint. He had seventy-nine men in his charge and, save for isolated incidents, discipline was remarkably good. This was made easier by Fowler's popularity among the men and his wisdom in keeping them occupied. Realizing that inactivity was the seed of discontent and mutiny, he made it his personal business to see that every man had something to fix his attention on. To this end he ordered the carpenter to take a number of men and begin the construction of two boats, one to be schooner- and the other sloop-rigged, with keels thirty-five feet long. The cutter was sent to the wreck of the *Cato* to bring in suitable timbers for the keels of both vessels. Sawyers were put to sawing out planks from the stumps of masts—an incredible labour—and the armourer to forging nails from scrap iron. Other parties were sent out to fish, and still others were detailed to assist the cooks.

So far there was nothing to complain of. They had not had time to become bored. Lieutenant Fowler wrote, after a meal of fresh fish washed down with Madeira:

> Were I a Poet I would describe the envy with which the Sea Gods must have beheld our invasion of their Domain. On these occasions our Companions in the *Bridgewater* did not receive our Blessings.

But always there hung over their heads a sword in the shape of a gale which would make the bank untenable. Bad weather could not hold off for ever. There was every incentive to industry, to hurry forward with the building of the boats. With so many hands the work proceeded rapidly. The keels were laid, and the sawyers were busy cutting out frames and planking. Cross-legged on the sand, the sail-makers sat plying palm and needle, and all day long the ring of the armourer's hammer could be heard as he made nails, angle-irons, and chain plates. In the evening after supper all except those on watch were excused further duty. A few crude games were devised, but the literate ones craved for books, the few volumes that had been saved being in great demand. Among the company was one who had some pretensions as an artist, who made a sketch of the camp, which was later reproduced in England as a steel engraving. Most evenings a drum-and-fife band played lively sailor airs, and this entertainment became very popular, the entire company joining in and singing.

September began with cloudy, windy weather, which was watched anxiously by the castaways. To their intense relief it cleared up within a few days, and they breathed easy again. A great deal of useful material, such as cordage and different-sized blocks, continued to be brought from the wreck of the *Porpoise*. The armourer now fell ill of some sort of fever, and shipbuilding was held up until he had sufficiently recovered to return to his forge. Another little disciplinary diversion occurred at this time. The drummer had been found asleep while sentinel over the stores, and, as an example to the rest, received half a dozen lashes. On September 6 a small raft was sent out to the *Porpoise*, and brought back a twelve-pound carronade, with several shot. Within two days all the guns had been brought ashore. There had lately been much rain, and several barrels had been filled by making large funnels of canvas. As the

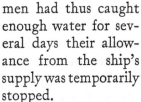

men had thus caught enough water for several days their allowance from the ship's supply was temporarily stopped.

Some of the men began to show signs of dejection, and even the cheerfullest spent much time gazing out to sea, hoping for a sight of the rescue ship. On September 12 Lieutenant Fowler went in the cutter to a bank which could be seen ten miles distant, where he and his crew stayed all night, returning to camp the next day. They described it as about three-quarters of a mile round, covered with rank grass and sea birds. They brought back two turtles, a quantity of eggs, and a number of birds. On the

14th Lieutenant Flinders was sent in charge of a boat to the bank, which had been dubbed Fowl Island, for more turtles, which were greatly liked as a change from the eternal salt pork and beef. On September 18 the custom was started of firing an evening gun as a signal to any vessel in the offing. The time allowance for Captain Flinders' return had nearly expired, and some openly voiced their uneasiness. Lieutenant Fowler wrote in his log a passage which I quote for the etymological interest of the phrase 'turn turtle.'

> Before Noon the next Day, I sent off the Master, Mr Aikin, and a Party to the Island, victualled for a week, *to turn Turtle*.

(The italics are mine.) After a week the party returned empty-handed, not having sighted one of these amphibians during their stay. Thirty-two days had passed since Captain Flinders had left, and most of the company believed that he had perished. Work was hurried forward on the two boats. As the coals were nearly exhausted a number of men were put to work breaking up the wreck for making charcoal for the armourer's forge. On October 5 the schooner was launched and christened *Resource*. A roomy boat, her dimensions were keel 35 feet, overall 37 feet, beam 12 feet 2 inches, and depth of hold 5 feet. After she was afloat the riggers got busy on her, while Chips superintended the laying down of keel of the sloop. On October 8 the cutter and the schooner were sent loaded with wood to Fowl Island with orders to burn charcoal there for the armourer. For some reason, probably lack of space, it was not convenient to burn charcoal on the sandbank. The boats got away at daybreak, and at noon, by which time the charcoal party would be on Fowl Island, the men on the sandbank saw, to their unspeakable joy, a square-rigged vessel and two smaller craft standing toward their refuge. The whole sandbank was at once in an uproar. Discipline, rules, flogging, and all minor tribulations were forgotten in the general expression of delight at the glorious sight seaward. Lieutenant Fowler,

153

at once dispatched the small cutter to Fowl Island to bring back the charcoal party. Charcoal had suddenly become a little ridiculous. At two-thirty in the afternoon the lieutenant went aboard the largest vessel, which was the *Rolla*, Robert Cummings master, where he learned that the two smaller craft were the *Francis* and *Cumberland*, schooners, with Captain Flinders on board the latter. The little squadron had been sent out to fetch them by order of the Governor of New South Wales.

Lieutenant Fowler, acting as pilot, conned the *Rolla* to an anchorage in twenty-two fathoms, one mile beyond the breakers. On going ashore he found that Captain Flinders had already landed, and ordered the people to embark on the *Rolla* as quickly as possible, and proceed with her to Canton, where, at the earliest opportunity, they would be conveyed either in a merchantman or a man-of-war, to England. The *Francis* was to return to Port Jackson with what stores from the sandbank she could carry, and such of the people as might desire their discharge. The charcoal party returned as soon as they heard of the arrival of the ships, and by the evening of the 9th most of the company were on board the *Rolla* with their sea-chests. But there was much to be done, a quantity of valuable stores to be got off the bank, and it was not until the 12th that every one was on board. Captain Flinders returned to Australia in the *Francis*.[1] Lieutenant Fowler went on the *Rolla* to accompany his men to England *via* Canton.

There remains nothing more to be told except the explanation of the mystery of the *Bridgewater*. This was publicly given through the medium of the *Madrass* [2] *Gazette*, dated December 31, 1803.

By the *Bridgewater*, Captain Palmer, lately arrived at Mangalore, we learn the following unfortunate occurrence:
While the *Bridgewater* was lying at Botany Bay, H.M. Ship

---

[1] I find another account says that he returned directly to England in the *Cumberland*.　　[2] Old Spelling.

Investigator, which had been temporarily employed on a Voyage of Discovery, arrived; and was obliged, from her state, to be condemned: the Captain and Crew were put on board the Transports, *Porpoise* and *Cato*, for the purpose of proceeding to Europe. The *Porpoise* and *Cato* and *Bridgewater* sailed in company from Port Jackson, and on the 18th of August the two former were wrecked; and we are concerned to add, that the whole of their Crews perished.

The report went on to say how the two ships were seen to crash on to the reef in the dark, and how the *Bridgewater* just cleared it. Captain Palmer stated that he at once held a consultation with his officers, and decided to stand off until daylight, feeling that it would be foolhardy to attempt to pick up any survivors in the dark. Thus he stood on and off throughout the remainder of the night, frequently harassed by heavy squalls. At daylight he saw the *Porpoise* nearly buried in the surf and the *Cato* even less visible. Captain Palmer argued that the weather remained too bad that day to attempt a rescue, but he continued to lie off until the following day, "when," and these are his own words,

> lying-to we again made the Reef and could see little or nothing of the Wreck of the *Porpoise* remaining; and the *Cato*, with her bottom exposed to a tremendous surf: Not a soul out of the two ships was it in our power to save.

From which report we are forced to think that Captain Palmer was guilty of neglect of his plain duty, which, as we see it, was to have approached close enough to be quite certain that not a soul remained alive. It is obvious that had he sailed in closer he would have seen the men on the sandbank, let alone those on the wreck. Fortunately his highly inaccurate report, which would have caused much needless grief in England, was forestalled by Captain Flinders reaching England first.

CHAPTER VIII

The Roistering Crusoes of Cargados Garayos

> To splinters was the vessel instant blown,
> The crash still adding to the tempest's roar;
> I saw my messmates, struggling, heard them groan,
> While, clinging to a plank, I gained the shore.
>
> *From an old ballad*

WHEN the Honourable East India Company's ship *Cabalva* left Gravesend for China, with a mixed cargo which included printed muslins, perfumery, soaps, and fancy goods, no one dreamed to what quaint uses this merchandise would shortly be put. The *Cabalva*, a 1200-ton ship, James Dalrymple commander, left the Thames in the month of April 1818, with a company of 130 men, all told, which included six officers, a surgeon, surgeon's mate, seven midshipmen, and one passenger bound for Canton. There were no women on board, which, in view of subsequent events, was fortunate. Besides the cargo already alluded to she carried a quantity of iron and lead, several cases of Spanish dollars, and, last of all, a score or so of casks of ale. Of this ale much more later. This is a suitable point to introduce the sixth officer, Mr C. W. Francken, with whom we will be in frequent contact during the exile upon the Cargados Reef and the subsequent boat journey in search of assistance. It is also to Mr Francken that we owe our knowledge of the strange events on the sandbank which came to be known as Beer Island.

The *Cabalva's* passage to the Cape of Good Hope was uneventful, and she had successfully weathered that stormy corner by the end of June, after a passage of two and a half months. The vast wastes of the Indian Ocean lay before the ship, and, by all the laws of chance, there was no reason why the *Cabalva* should not make the traverse without any untoward event happening. Nevertheless, on Monday, July 6, Captain Dalrymple was uneasy about the ship, and during the early hours of Tuesday ordered the officer on duty to keep a good look-out, and, as an additional precaution, sent two men aloft, one at each foreyard arm, in addition to a man at either cathead. Thus five men were keeping a special look-out ahead, an unusual demonstration of prudence, to be sure, but then Captain Dalrymple was unusually worried about his position, and seemed to have a premonition of some unseen danger.

It was then 4 A.M., Mr Francken's watch, and the sea and sky one in blackness, the moon having set an hour before, though the stars could be seen. It was a mild night; the men lay about in odd corners in the waist, asleep; the ship was under easy sail, as was the custom with Indiamen every night. She was making about seven and a half sea miles per hour, and, save for the slight hiss of the seas breaking on her bows and the shrill cry of sea-gulls overhead, quiet reigned. About four-thirty the watch was startled by a harsh shout from one of the look-out forward—the almost classic cry of danger at sea—"Breakers on the larboard bow!" followed by a second cry, "Hard aport!" repeated twice, thrice, in a rising *crescendo*.

But even as the lively Mr Francken ran aft to the wheel the ship's keel grated along a submerged rock, and she lost all forward way. Now some hitherto unfelt swell, the outer *tremolo* of breakers which could be heard thundering in the blackness, shook the unfortunate ship so violently against the hard reef that her sticks trembled like palms in a gale, and her wheel spun madly, throwing the quartermaster off like a drop of water from a spinning top. The violence of the motion of the hull at the same time hurled one of the look-outs off a yardarm into the sea, where he was drowned. This much within the first few seconds, so rapid was the transition from order to chaos. The sleeping men below were suddenly awakened by being flung violently out of their hammocks. Within less than a minute after the crash the upper decks were crowded with bewildered, frightened, and half-clad men, who had escaped drowning below to chance death from falling spars and gear overhead. The calm serenity of a stilly night had become a bedlam of shouts, of cracking, splintering wood and falling gear, with the thunder of not-far-distant breakers in the background. Noise, terror, pandemonium; so momentous, so serious for the ship and the men, and so trivial to the stars which looked down on the scene.

After what seemed a long time, though in reality but a few minutes, the officers won some sort of ascendancy over the terrified and bewildered crew, and ordered the masts to be instantly cut away. Some ran for the rigging with hatchets, others cut deep notches in the great boles themselves, until, one after another, they crashed overside, carrying with them the heavy yards and gear. With the sacrifice of the masts and spars the ship immediately ceased most of her violent motions, and as dawn was now breaking it became possible to get the cutter overside without mishap. Carrying several officers, the surgeon, and the Canton passenger, she was headed for a low reef visible in the grey light of early morning. Captain Dalrymple and Mr Francken appeared to be the sole members of the afterguard left on the ship. But there was no question of reproaching the deserters. When a situation seems as hopeless as this seemed, with no choice betwixt the ship and the boats, it becomes a case of *sauve qui peut*—and the devil take those who do not help themselves!

Mr Francken, now left to his own devices, crawled forward to examine the position and condition of the wreck, and found her to be lying across a sunken reef, her back broken, and her poop and fo'c'sle only above the water. In the half light he could make out a number of men feebly swimming near the wreck, and in great peril of being crushed by the floating spars all round them. To leeward could be seen another boat, the large cutter carrying thirty odd men, and yawning dangerously in the giant combers crashing on the reef. Watching, he saw her shudder as she struck a rock, fill with water, and spill her company into the sea. The

surgeon's mate, a Mr Grant, being a strong swimmer, now decided to take his chance and dived overboard. At first he struck out vigorously for the reef, but before reaching it was seen to throw up his arms and sink. There remained still the longboat, the heaviest boat in the ship, which for that reason, had not been launched. If it could be got afloat there might be a chance of riding the breakers safely, and Mr Francken decided to make the attempt. Handicapped by the absence of spars from which to launch the boat and the depth of water amidships, the task proved Herculean, but there was no lack of man-power, and in the end the heavy craft floated. Into her climbed twenty men besides the captain and the ubiquitous Francken, but before she could clear the wreckage near the ship she was stove by a floating spar, and every man found himself in the water again. There began a free-for-all race for the nearest visible rocks, which lay not over 150 yards away. Up on the sides and crests of the giant combers the helpless men floated like a number of detached fish-net corks, bracing themselves for the perilous moment when they would be dashed to pieces or gently floated ashore. One ingenious fellow was seen to be using a bale of cloth from the wreck as a buffer for his body as he approached the threatening rocks. Of the company which had been spilt out of the longboat, some had regained the ship, some the reef, while others had been

drowned. There were between eighty and ninety men now on the wreck; among these were Mr Francken and Captain Dalrymple, half-dressed in a pair of flannel drawers and a pea-jacket, as he had rushed up from his cabin at the ship's first striking. From down below in his own *sanctum sanctorum* he could hear the sailors making merry with his private wine store, but he made no attempt to stop them. The imminence of death had stunned him, and he left things pretty much in the hands of the young and vigorous Francken.

This officer was meanwhile making another effort to get the patched-up longboat away in a second attempt to reach the reef. But no sooner had a crowd of men got in her than she was for a second time holed, drowning five of the company. Some others had managed to lash a number of spars together to form a kind of raft, and, as this was floating near, Francken was able to climb on to it and pull the half-

drowned captain on also. On this badly articulated float
Francken, the captain, two midshipmen, and about eighteen
seamen rode shoreward with no steering oar or other means
of keeping the raft from broaching to in the valleys between
the seas. And as it approached the last breakers it swung
broadside to the surf and capsized, falling on the hapless
men, rolling men and spars over violently in a giant roly-
poly. Fighting for air, some with broken ribs, the raft's.
company were hurled on to the rocks, and when the survivors
were counted the captain was missing. A popular skipper,
his death cast a gloom over the survivors. On this rock the
raft's crew found a number of others crouched shivering
and dejected among the flotsam thrown up by the dismem-
bered *Cabalva*. Mr Francken landed stark naked, and, seeing
his plight, a seaman named William Maddem retrieved some
odd pieces of clothing for him, a service which Francken
never forgot. And from somewhere the humane seaman
produced a mug of beer, which put the officer further in
his debt.

There were still on the wreck the fifth officer and half a
dozen seamen, who later came off in the dead captain's gig.
Sharing the rock with the castaways were the bruised, white
corpses of a number of their late shipmates. So far as a
hasty roll-call could establish 110 men were alive. About
twenty or thereabouts had been drowned. The purser,
doctor, passenger, and officers were all saved. Now, as the
tide receded with the advancing morning the reef rose out
of the sea, and left in its jagged crannies was all manner of
wreckage strewn about in untidy confusion. There were
scores of bales of brightly coloured cloths, muslins, cretonne,
dimity, and casks, cases, spars, trunks, and chests. Recovering in the friendly warmth of the sun, the seamen grew
loud-mouthed and unruly, and, acting on the principle of
each for himself, pillaged the wreckage, ripping open the
cloth bales and staving the beer-casks. In taking the cloth
they had reason on their side, for now the tropical sun,

riding high in a blazing sky, became only tolerable if the
body was protected from its direct rays. And, being more
or less naked, the men swathed themselves in the protecting
cloth, until they made up the motliest crowd of castaways
ever seen on a desert shore. In every direction on the
uncovered, pool-dotted coral reef could be seen gaily clad
figures, many recklessly drunk. Some of the sober ones were
attempting hurriedly to construct a raft in anticipation of

high water, when it was thought the reef would be covered
by the sea. One little group was trying to stop up the seams
of a damaged boat, and here and there hungry ones searched
shallow pools for shellfish.

The officers seem to have been mainly engaged in knock-
ing in the heads of beer-casks and making an effort to
restore some sort of order. The majority of the seamen
were quite helplessly drunk, and if the tide inundated the
rock they must be surely drowned, as they no longer had
wits enough to man the boats. However, the thought of
the tide soon returning had a sobering effect on all but the
worst of the tipsy men, and a general trek was begun toward
a bank of sand standing, at the highest point, perhaps five

feet above the sea. Accompanied by half a dozen sailors, each clutching a wine-bottle, Mr Francken walked barefooted over uneven rocks, sometimes waist high in water, toward the distant sandbank. On the way he caught a young shark, which he dragged along with him, a slimy unpalatable dead thing, but worth more than gold.

Arriving at the sandbank, he found it to be about 140 yards long by about 80 yards wide, and already occupied

by a motley crowd of men drunk and sober, and ludicrous to look upon. Some wore turbans of flowered calico twisted about their heads, others swaggered in fancy caps and bonnets which had been destined for trade in China. Their feet were clumsy with muslin, or skins swathed and tied, for there was not a single pair of shoes among them. All had abundance of wine and brandy, which they nursed even as they slept sprawled on the sand. Others were quarrelling, or larking, boxing, chasing each other, or catching the sea birds, who, it may be, were too astonished at what they saw to fly away. Here they were, cast upon a low reef, totally inadequate to support life, out of the ship-track in the Southern Indian Ocean, in a desperate situation, and they were skylarking! The young but sober-minded sixth officer looked at this astonishing sight a little sadly, and wondered if he could find enough clear-headed men to return with him to the wreck for food and fresh water. So he went among them, talking to them, pointing out their peril, but found them ready only to argue the point, to stare at him with lack-lustre eyes, and to begin a befuddled harangue. Utterly worn out, Mr Francken lay down and slept.

He awoke some time later to find others had joined the original group. The sandbank was crowded with men. Some had had the foresight to bring food such as salved pork, and from somewhere had been brought three leather buckets of fresh water. With a dozen bottles of wine, the young shark, and a few lobsters caught in the pools, a hundred men made their first meal on the reef. Some ingenious fellow had got a fire going by striking a razor against a piece of glass, the spark falling into a shred of dry rag sprinkled with gunpowder. As the afternoon advanced the tide rose and covered the rocks where the men had first found refuge, but, to the unspeakable relief of the sober ones, did not cover the sandbank. As the sea rose it lifted everything floatable that scattered the reef and swept it on to the sandbank, which lay three miles to leeward of the wreck. Until dark a score or so of the men busied themselves retrieving from the surf the miscellaneous, and mostly useless, flotsam. A besotted sailor would bellow with tipsy mirth as he picked up a case of pomatum or a box of stationery, but others felt the irony of these finds. Lavender-water, perfumed soap, hair, tooth- and clothes-brushes, and beads—what comfort for hungry and destitute men! But from the bolts of printed muslins and Irish linen a crazy sort of tent was contrived (spread on broken spars), and into this shelter crept thirty or forty of the more wilful spirits, leaving their officers and leaders to spend the night in the open as best they could. One of the boats, the large cutter, which had been hauled thirty yards over the reef, and now lay moored close to the wreck, served to house nine men, who spent a restless and wearisome night in her.

The next morning, July 8, all the sober men agreed that the stores and drink should be put in charge of responsible officers and rationed out in small quantities. While the rowdy faction were in the majority, they offered no serious resistance to this proposal The first breakfast was so slight— two ounces of pork and a dram of beer—that some of the feckless ones suddenly saw for the first time the seriousness of their position, and joined the others in forming parties to retrieve stores from the wreckage, the stronger fellows to wade or swim to the wreck for the cutter and whatever useful they could get out of her, especially casks of water. Another party was sent to a neighbouring sandbank (there were many glistening white in the sunlight at low tide) to bring over what they could of a number of barrels and cases which could be seen lying on the sand. Still others, mainly those with wounded feet, stayed 'at home,' enlarging the tent and setting up a flagstaff for a distress signal. Bolts of cloth were unrolled and spread in long, gaudy ribbons on the hot sand to dry. But, in the face of all this industry for the common weal, there were a large number of lazy and quarrelsome men who hung about and refused to work.

That morning the wreck party, under Mr Sewell, chief officer, made a heartening discovery, when, after wading for hours up to their waists over uneven rocks, they came upon the longboat, abandoned and loaded with a glorious treasure of provisions and merchandise. Lying in a sodden jumble between the thwarts of the boat were twelve dead fowls, a drowned sheep, one large pine cheese, mixed up with fire-arms, cutlery, wine, watches, dollars, and muslin. So great was the discoverers' delight at finding the boat intact, and with all this treasure, that they had failed at first to notice a human occupant lying on his back in the stern-sheets, bemoaning a hurt leg, which was swathed gigantically in layers of bright muslin. Mr Francken's story becomes at times unconsciously Gilbertian, as here, for instance, in describing the work of salvage near the wreck. The fifth officer, who bemoaned a broken leg when he had nothing of the kind, was put into a grog tub (they were large, shallow affairs), and pushed ashore, his swathed leg sticking out aggressively. Mr Francken did the pushing, while another man guided inshore the lid of a chest, on which lay grunting a live pig that had been taken in tow as it floated by on its little raft. Accompanying the grog tub and the 'raft,' with their respective passengers, were three or four seamen, wading waist deep, and dragging with them three live pigs and two live sheep. Around the men's necks hung muskets, pistols, and a number of drowned fowls, all taken from the wreck.

On the return Mr Sewell discovered that there had been a conspiracy among those who had spent the night in the cutter to steal away in an attempt to reach some inhabited island, or, if possible, the mainland of Africa, which lay somewhere to the westward. A foolhardy plot, since they possessed neither oars, sail, compass, nor rudder, nor any plan of navigating her, and would most inevitably have perished, apart from the fact that the loss of the cutter would have been fatal to those left behind.

At five in the afternoon Francken reached the sandbank with his groaning patient in the grog tub, who was tenderly carried ashore and put in charge of the surgeon. This bluff fellow unwound the numerous wrappings, examined the leg, and, despite the patient's protests to the contrary, swore that there was positively nothing wrong with his leg.

An hour later the chief officer arrived with the longboat heavily laden with further stores taken from the wreck. The boat's crew were worn out with dragging the heavy craft three miles over sand and rock. With the arrival of this party the entire company were piped for supper, a feast consisting of another dram of beer and two ounces each of the drowned fowls. Those in charge of the commissariat were determined to husband the stores, which now consisted of half a dozen live pigs, five sheep, two dozen dead fowls, fifty pieces of pork and beef, a small keg of flour, three casks of beer, four dozen bottles of wine and one dozen of cherry brandy, five pine cheeses, but neither biscuits nor water. Later a salvage party brought in an additional twenty pieces of salt pork.

Among other things salved was a sextant, a quadrant, a soaked copy of Horsburgh's *Sailing Directions*, and Norie's *Navigation*, as well as several muskets, pistols, cutlasses, knives, forks, spoons, plates, and a frying-pot. Farquharson, caulker's mate, who had conducted himself with exemplary courage during the morning of the wreck, returned in the evening from a long journey. His account of his doings was evasive and unsatisfactory, but it was learned that he had wandered miles over the sand reefs, which, he stated, were littered with wreckage. That night the first guard was set up, and the officers took the watches, the orders being (1) to watch the tide at its flow, (2) to look out for ships, and (3) to guard the provision dump. Those on guard were to be armed with a pistol, and were to shoot anyone approaching within five paces. The night proved chilly and rainy, and the watch had a wretched time, for they were without shelter of any kind.

On the third day the business of putting their house in order proceeded smoothly without any active obstruction from the recalcitrant element. The sober and well helped the drunk and the sick. Many were suffering agonies from feet gashed on the sharp coral, and now found the despised pomatum a soothing dressing, the foot being then wrapped in a muslin bandage. The carpenter and his mates began to repair the damaged cutter, and the sailmaker, whose bag, containing needles and palm, was providentially among the flotsam washed ashore, set to work making sails. The bos'n exercised his skill at making rope by twisting three strips of muslin together. Parties returning from the wreck reported

167

that the poop and fo'c'sle had driven in a hundred yards
nearer the rocks, and that in the cuddy they had found a
sailor flat on his face in a drunken sleep. He had been
brought ashore on a raft along with a quantity of sail rope
and several dozen bottles of wine. As they had found the
captain's boat, albeit much damaged, near the wreck, they
had loaded their stuff (including the drunken sailor) into it,
and dragged it over to the sandbank. They told of having

met two tipsy seamen wading in the shallows near the wreck,
wrangling over their loot. One held out a hatful of watches,
seals, rings, and other trinkets, while the other, whose muslin
cummerbund was stuffed with Spanish dollars, bickered for
a gold watch, offering four dollars, "not a peso more."
"I'll see you damned first," retorted the other muzzily,
toppling perilously forward. So the other grandly offered
twice as much, but they must needs argue, and, feeling this
insufficient, the one with the hatful of watches put it down
upon a rock while the pair of them fought it out.

This day's salvage was encouraging. The captain's boat
was greeted with huzzas, and dragged close up to the two
tents. The stores brought in amounted to four butts of
fresh water, a like number of beer, three dozen of wine, forty
pieces of salt pork and beef, a drowned and half-decayed
pig, and more canvas and cordage. The chief officer stated
that he had left on another sandbank sixteen mutinous and

intoxicated seamen, with whom he could do nothing. He also announced that he had buried five dead men, one being much like the captain, *though of this he could not be sure as the head was missing*. The ring finger was also missing. He had heard that the digit had been bitten off by one of the mutinous men in order to secure a gold ring.

The carpenters, sailmakers, and bos'n continued at their work reconditioning the large cutter, while parties visited the wreck and surrounding reefs at low tide in search of anything edible or useful. The number of inefficient had noticeably decreased, and two-thirds of the company were now pulling their weight. The lack of clothes encouraged many to try their hand at tailoring, canvas and calico being the stock material for the crude garments laboriously sewn together. Mr Sewell and Mr Francken set out early exploring the sandbanks in search of provisions. After a two hours' walk, up to their necks in water or over dry sand, they came to the island of the mutineers. The camp was picturesque if nothing else. Inside a semicircle beyond reach of the tide, a semicircle made of up-ended casks of beer, stood a number of tiny tents, or shelters, of printed muslin, each tent placed up against a beer-cask in such a way that the occupant, lying prone, could guzzle without the necessity of stirring out of his shelter. They seemed to have very little food, but this did not appear to worry them greatly so long as the beer lasted. In keeping with his swashbuckling air each man was festooned with as many weapons as he could find—pistols, cutlasses, muskets, and even carving-knives. For the most part they wore nothing more than a piece of muslin swathed round their middles and another piece round their heads, turban-wise. The muskets were slung to a strip of cloth arranged as a bandolier over the shoulder, and from each bravo's belt hung a bottle of wine. They strutted about, bronzed and dirty, quite unconscious of the comic aspect of their present existence. While the two officers were there a brace of the precious rascals, both gloriously drunk, rolled about in the sand, fighting for possession of a gold inlaid fowling-piece. The others, accustomed to such sights, paid small attention to this diversion.

The visitors returned to their own camp with one of the roisterers, the surgeon's mate, sobered by a hand badly

wounded through the bursting of a gun barrel, and now ready to join the other camp for the sake of the medical attention he would get. But we must not be too hard on the secessionists. They civilly permitted the visiting officers to drink with them, though they could not offer any food. Nearly the whole of their sandbank was submerged at high tide, making their position extremely dangerous; but, living constantly in the rosy atmosphere of their cups, why should they worry? On the way back Mr Francken spoke of them as " the Beer Island Gang," and the name stuck for ever after. At night their camp was marked out by an enormous fire of driftwood, which would die down as the revellers fell asleep. The main party kept a fire going all night, tended by the watch, on the remote chance that it might be sighted by a distant ship.

On Saturday, July 11, the officers worked out the position, and calculated that the nearest inhabited land was Mauritius, south-west by south, distance 250 miles. They were on the Cargados Garayos Bank, north-east by north of Mauritius. A conference was held which resulted in the decision to send the large cutter with a few picked men and an officer to Mauritius, Bourbon, or Madagascar, whichever place the wind favoured. This day was also distinguished by the finding of water by digging deep in the sand.

The camp had by now settled down into a disciplined routine, the steward, whose job was an unpopular and thankless one, scrupulously doling out two ounces of meat and a dram of beer twice a day, at 7 A.M. and 6 P.M. It required the entire day to cut up the meat in equal proportions and to care for the livestock. The sheep were fortunate in receiving a ration of hay from a bale which had been washed ashore, but the pigs had to be content with beer grounds and an *à la carte* choice of scented soap or pomatum! Tents had been contrived out of canvas or muslin sufficient to house every one, and from a description of the officers' tent one imagines they had made themselves quite cosy—a home from home, in fact. The tent, which was about ten feet high, was made of strips of red and blue cloth stretched over ridge-poles, from which hung two 'elegant' globe lamps holding wax candles. The sandy floor was covered with the ubiquitous muslin, and was untidily littered with little white jars of Naples soap and pomatum, pens, pencils, stationery, brushes, combs, and other miscellaneous and useless trifles. The Spanish dollars and gold watches formerly so much in evidence had disappeared. A wooden chest in one corner contained the nautical instruments, tables, and *cheese*! All the wine and brandy was buried in the sand beneath the floor-cloths. From the ridge-pole hung the muskets and side-arms. The fifth officer lay on another chest all day nursing his 'wounded leg,' which he kept swathed in "at least eight pieces of muslin." Another lay on his back all day, seldom opening his mouth except to eat or complain of his wretchedness. He had found a copy of *Rob Roy*, or half a copy, since the second volume was missing from among the wreckage, and complained that he could not finish it. When the second volume was discovered to be with the Beer Island Gang an attempt was made to obtain it legitimately, but these fellows were unwilling to part with it. The Canton passenger, known simply as Mr H., was regarded enviously, he being the possessor of not only a shirt, shoes, and trousers, but also a hat, coat, and a snuff-box. Some remarked that he did not appear to be particularly grateful for his good fortune, a species of human frailty we seem to have come across not infrequently.

On Sunday, July 12, the main party was favoured by a visit from twelve of the Beer Islanders, led by a fourteen-year-old midshipman, who had been with them since the beginning. They had come somewhat sheepishly, with black eyes and flesh wounds requiring medical attention. The boy, who had learned quickly from his elders, boasted that they had plenty of fish, beer, and wine, and that one of the foretop men had been elected chaplain, reading them prayers every night. He admitted that the gang spent the day drinking, sporting, fishing, and fighting, and that, for sweet prudence' sake, he slept in an empty water-butt. This Sunday Mr Ayres, the purser, delivered a discourse to the whole company assembled round the longboat, bidding the men be of good cheer, pious and obedient, and their leaders would bring them to civilization in due time.

On the Monday the boat was pronounced ready for sea,

but few realized what difficulties had been surmounted to make it so. When the names of the chosen crew were written and stuck up for every one to read it was seen that Mr Francken was to be in charge, with Mr Ayres second in command. Eight seamen were chosen—Martin, McKenzie, Colley, Austin, Duncan, Edwards, Henderson, and Johnson.[1] It was proposed to keep the boat close upon a wind —the trades blew in this quarter within about four points of south-east by east—until she should reach the latitude of Mauritius; then bear up and keep her head due west. That is as near as possible without a compass! Sailors will appreciate this. The boat was to carry two none too reliable watches, a quadrant,[2] a log reel, and Norie's *Epitome of Practical Navigation.* Just before leaving Mr Francken was greatly touched by the present of a pair of trousers one the seamen had made for him. These, as the recipient said, added greatly to his comfort. For provisions the boat was provided with four pieces of pork, twenty flour-and-water cakes, a pine cheese, eight gallons of water, and three bottles of brandy. She carried a lug sail,[3] eight oars, baling buckets, some muskets and powder, and was ballasted with bales of cloth! Mr Francken intended to try first for Mauritius, and, failing that, either Bourbon or Madagascar. He was excused his watch this last night ashore, since heaven only knew when he would sleep again.

I was excused from keeping watch this night, and took a walk round the sandbank about eleven o'clock quite by myself, it being a very beautiful evening. My companions were asleep in their tents except the watch officer, who is stirring the fire and gathering fuel round the beach; the roaring of breakers overwhelms the crackling and blazing noise of the flames; the sky is totally clear; the moon, in the act of setting, throws a pale lustre over the level surface of the sea that extends towards the west, unlimited except

---

[1] Some versions give a total of eleven men.
[2] Another version denies Francken a quadrant.
[3] One account states there were three masts.

by the horizon. Towards the north an endless chain of low sand-banks, and, at a considerable distance in that direction, the watch-fire of the mutineers. Towards the south and east nothing but breakers, occupying the horizon like an immense wall of water, and showing the wretched remains of the *Cabalva* now and then between white, splashing foam.

Near by lay the cutter, which stood between life or death for the castaways, ready for her 250-mile journey—*sans* compass. Mr Francken's position might aptly be compared with that of Shackleton, who stood looking at the *James Caird* on the eve of his departure from Elephant Island in 1916.

July 14, the momentous day, arrived, and the whole camp assembled on the beach to witness the boat's departure at 5 A.M. Her crew had been given a more substantial meal than usual, to start them off a little less jaded than might be. With hoarse cheers the little ship of hope was pushed off, and with sail filling she scudded before the wind until clear of the reefs and breakers, when, close-reefed, she was hauled upon a wind, and began the voyage in earnest. The short, jerky motion of the boat soon made every one violently sick, a misfortune which had its benefits, since it helped conserve the scanty store of food. The weather became squally, but they were able to keep to their course all day, travelling at an average of six knots. Sleep that night was impossible owing to the motion of the boat and the constant shipping of water. Every one had to assist at baling throughout the night. The sky was clear, and the southern constellations aided navigation considerably.

The second morning the sea was calmer, and at noon an observation was made after heaving-to for the purpose. Every one believed Mauritius would be raised the next day, a faith that was justified, for at dawn on the third morning a faint adumbration of land was seen to the south. It was recognized as Round Island, close to Mauritius. By noon they were abreast of Port Louis, but, alas, fourteen miles to leeward. As it was impossible to beat to windward, the sail

STANLEY ROGERS

"BEGAN THE VOYAGE IN EARNEST"

was taken in and the oars shipped for a long pull to the land. Progress was so slow, however, that the canvas was again set. Darkness would soon be on them, and the men grew alarmed at the prospect of being blown to sea during the night. At sunset a miraculous slant of wind from the right quarter enabled them to work inshore, and shortly after the anchor was dropped in nine feet of water. Here they remained, sheltering under the sail as best they could in a pouring rain, until 4 A.M., when they raised the anchor and rowed four miles along the coast to Port Louis, where they were received with a mixture of curiosity and kindliness by the islanders, who stared amazed at the strangely garbed castaways, each an odd mixture of pirate, clown, and savage. They were plied with questions while they were given coffee, bread, and fresh fruits.

Mr Ayres, as purser, reported at once to the East India Company's agent, who promptly communicated the facts of the wreck to the captain of H.M. frigate *Magicienne*. This officer acted with such dispatch that within an hour the frigate was unmoored and proceeding to the rescue of the castaways, with Mr Francken, Mr Ayres, and two of their men on board, accompanied by the brig *Challenger*. In boisterous weather the frigate stood south with four eager volunteer pilots to guarantee her course. On Sunday, July 20, breakers were seen on the starboard bow, and a little later the thin reed of a flagstaff was made out. Captain Purvis, of the *Magicienne*, ordered a salute of gunfire every ten minutes, which was answered from the reef by the jubilant Crusoes letting off quantities of gunpowder. So the happily brief sojourn on Cargados Garayos Reef was brought to an end.

As for the men on the reefs, the Beer Island Gang had, toward the end, increased in numbers, but so long as their beer and wine lasted the other party felt no uneasiness about them. As far as could be made out, they appeared to live principally on turtles' eggs. On account of continuous stormy weather since the large cutter had left, those behind gave her up for lost, and formed a plan to sail northward in the captain's boat in search of a higher bank. When the frigate was sighted the company was assembled at prayers. The bos'n's wandering eyes saw the distant sail, and, instantly forgetting their devotions, the whole company ran to the water's edge, shouting and cheering. Every one went temporarily mad with joy, and for a while the Lord of Misrule reigned over the scene. Stores were pillaged, tents destroyed, gunpowder fired,[1] men hugged each other, some did a *pas seul* or playfully fought with others, but a few fell flat on their faces in devout thankfulness for their deliverance.

The work of getting them off was safely carried out despite the high seas running, and before long the sedate decks of the frigate were swarming with the fantastically clad Crusoes. The ship looked as though she had been boarded by a company of pirates. The Beer Island Gang had hurried to join the main party as soon as the frigate hove in sight, and now they appeared, besotted, and not one whit penitent for their conduct. Indeed, they loudly bewailed the necessity of leaving so much good beer behind. It is of interest to note that their insubordination was overlooked by the East India Company officials, who deemed it useless to attempt to punish these feckless men. All the castaways were transferred to the *Challenger*, with the exception of Chief Officer Sewell, who remained behind in the frigate in an attempt to salvage some of the *Cabalva's* more valuable cargo. All on the reef had sworn never to go to sea again if they lived to reach civilization, but this vow was not kept. Most of the seamen shipped immediately they could get berths.

Mr Francken arrived in England on November 21 in the

---

[1] When Shackleton's twenty-two men, marooned on Elephant Island in the Antarctic in 1916, saw the rescue ship approaching one of them drove a pick into their last precious tin of fuel and set it on fire.

Free-trader *Orient*, as third mate. The following letter from the East India Company is self-explanatory:

EAST INDIA HOUSE
19th of February, 1819

SIR,

I have received the commands of the Court of Directors of the East India Company to acquaint you that they have resolved to present you with the sum of Fifty Guineas, and a sextant, with the Company's arms, and a suitable inscription engraved upon it; as a mark of their approbation of your meritorious conduct on the occasion of your proceeding from the Cargados Reef to the Mauritius in an open boat, to the speedy arrival of which at that place, the early relief and preservation of the crew of the late ship *Cabalva* may be mainly attributed.

I am, Sir,
Your most humble and obedient Servant,
J. DART
Secretary

Mr C. W. FRANCKEN

CHAPTER IX

Polar Crusoes

Let Greenland's snows
Then shine, and mark the melancholy train
There left to perish, whilst the cold, pale day
Declines along the farther ice, that binds
The ship, and leaves in night the sinking scene.
W. L. BOWLES, *The Spirit of Discovery*

A SKIN-CLAD Crusoe posing against a background of waving palms and a cerulean sky is not an unfamiliar picture, but a skin-clad Crusoe against cold, white ice and a leaden sky is less easily visualized. To choose an ice-floe for a Crusoe adventure would be surely exhibiting shockingly bad judgment, not to mention a sad breach of tradition. For the traditional Crusoe should never stray beyond the generous limits of the tropics of Cancer and Capricorn, where he is assured of a reasonably habitable climate, to say the least. But there is no accounting for the Goddess of Chance, and when men venture far among the Polar ice they are tempting her to betray them. The tales of these Crusoes of the Great Cold were more common in the past times than they happen to be in the present age, when we know better how to protect ships against the ice, and when we have the advantage of wireless and the aeroplane.

Hakluyt, Purchas, and Churchill all give us records of

Polar Crusoes, though they are not described as such. In 1774 the Royal Society of London caused to be printed a translation from the German of a remarkable document describing the experiences of four Russian sailors who were cast away on the bleak and barren island of East Spitsbergen in the year 1743. The narrative was first published (in German) in St Petersburg by a professor of history, M. Le Roy, in 1768, six years before the Royal Society had it translated.

In 1743 Jeremiah [1] Okladmkoff, a merchant of Mezen in the province of Jugovia, Government of Archangel, fitted out a ship for a whaling and sealing voyage to Spitsbergen. Sailing with a crew of fourteen men, the little whaler bowled along for eight days with a fair wind until Browne Island, Spitsbergen, was raised. When within three versts [2] of the land the ship was beset by ice, and the captain held a conference with his men in order to decide what best to do. The vessel lay in a position of great peril, and when the mate, Alexis Himkoff, suggested that they should drag their stores over the ice and winter ashore there was no dissenting voice, for the reason that there was no other choice, since to stay in the ship would have been suicidal. As Alexis said he had been told that there was a hut on the island where the party could winter, four men, Alexis Himkoff, Ivan Himkoff, Stephen Scharapoff, and Feodor Weregin, with light loads, muskets, powder and ball, axe, small kettle, bag of flour, knife, tinder-box, and tobacco, packed in bags, walked across the two miles of loose-pressure ice to the shore, to investigate the reality of the rumoured hut. After some little search it was seen standing among the grey rocks one and a half miles from the shore—a large wooden cabin thirty-six feet long by eighteen feet wide by eighteen feet high, with a small annex twelve feet square. There was one outside door to the larger cabin, the only entrance to the smaller structure being by a communicating door between the two. In the main room stood a large earthenware oven minus a

---

[1] This is the English spelling.   [2] About two miles.

BEYOND THE ARCTIC CIRCLE

chimney. Happy at the discovery of these commodious quarters, the four men—as it was now late in the day—. decided to spend the night here, and return to the ship in the morning. Not being provided with bedding, they passed a wretchedly cold night, and were up early the next morning to hurry down to the shore and board the ship with the good tidings. They counted on making several journeys over the ice that day with stores from the ship, for, with the floes crushing the vessel, no time must be lost in getting the necessary provisions and gear safely out of her.

Imagine, then, the blank disappointment of these four men when, on coming down to the shore, they found the bay free of ice and the ship nowhere in sight. Where the day before had lain a field of ice as far as the eye could see there was now open water. The men remembered that the wind had blown a gale during the night, but had expected nothing like this. There was no means of knowing whether the ship was lost or not. One thought so, another thought not. In any event, a few days at the most would tell. It was inconceivable that the captain would sail away without them. If the wind had carried the ice-bound ship out to sea she would be able, if not sunk, to work back to the land. There was nothing to do but wait, but if she did not re-appear the position of the four men would be serious. Their only food was twenty pounds of flour, and their ammunition sufficient for twelve charges.

With true Slavonic emotionalism, they allowed the discovery to plunge them into the depths of despair. They cursed the fates that had abandoned them to slow and horrible deaths, alone and forgotten in the northern cold. The shock at first rendered them incapable of action, and for a long time they remained, drooping figures of despair, gazing dully out to sea, where a few hours before stood the ship, the bridge between life and death. So it seemed. But the same mercurial temperament that threw them into despondency now raised them to hope. There was the cabin; there were twelve charges of powder and ball; and perhaps the ship had survived and would return. Meanwhile there would be plenty to do, making the hut habitable and securing food. The walls of the building were gaping with wide cracks, and the roof was beginning to show the ravages of winters of neglect. But these Russian peasants were good carpenters, and repairs were by no means difficult. As for the cracks, nothing could be better than moss—of which there was an abundance—to stuff them with. Moss or clay is the time-honoured method of filling in the spaces between the logs of log-cabins the world over, as anyone who has helped build this type of structure knows. One of my own earliest recollections is of myself, as a child of four or five, pushing moss in between the cedar logs of my father's cabin in the Black Hills, which are a spur of the Cascade Range in North-western Washington.

The cold was already intense, and the first problem, after making the hut windproof, was to contrive some way of keeping a fire. But how? There were neither trees nor shrubs on the island, but fortunately there was plenty of driftwood along the beach, and a quantity was at once collected and laboriously hauled the mile and a half inland to the cabin. Most of the driftwood, however, was too large (being whole trees or timbers of ships) to drag to the cabin in one piece, and had to be chopped into convenient lengths before it could be moved. Meanwhile the best marksmen would go off to stalk reindeer, and, by exercising great care, not a grain of the precious powder was wasted, the twelve charges accounting for the same number of deer.

On the beach, while engaged in collecting driftwood, a board, in which was fixed a long iron hook and a number of nails, was found. This unexciting object roused in its discovery a most immoderate demonstration of joy, as though they had found El Dorado. And well they might be overjoyed, for just then an old piece of iron was of more use to the castaways than a regiment of Golden Men. Heating it, and other pieces of iron attached to the board, in their fire, they were able to forge a hammer and several lance-heads. With the ammunition gone, it was imperative to possess some weapon of defence against the white bears, which were known to be dangerous enemies to men. A bow was also made from the root of a derelict spruce-tree. With such artificial aids, fangless, clawless man put himself on more equal terms with his naturally armed, hereditary enemy, *Ursus maritimus*. For an anvil a large stone served, and on other stones were ground the forged weapons, lance- and arrow-heads, which were afterward securely lashed to sticks with wet deer thongs. These in drying shrink, and so make the lashing extraordinarily tight.

When in time (for the ship never came back) the deer meat was consumed the men went hunting their first Polar bear, armed with nothing but spears. The four hungry and desperate men, armed with stout lances, were more than a match for the bear, and choice cuts of its flesh were soon boiling over a fire. And those who have tasted bear steak can vouch for its resemblance to beef, albeit somewhat tougher, for your bear is an active and muscular animal. The first Bruin supplied the sinews for a cord to the crude bow made from the spruce root. With confidence gained from their initial success as primitive hunters, the castaways unhesitatingly attacked and slew other bears, thus ensuring clothes and food. Their arrows were works of art—strong, slender shafts tipped with iron sharpened on stones to a razor edge, and feathered from the plumage of sea-birds. With this weapon no less than 250 reindeer and a large number of blue and white foxes were killed during their exile on the island. The bears, their only dangerous enemy, were not killed so easily, it being necessary to attack them at close quarters with spears. The fact that only ten were slain during the six years on the island suggests something of the difficulties and hazards of this method of bear-hunting.

I said that they spent six years in this solitude. They spent longer—six years and three months to be exact! At that date East Spitsbergen might have been the North Pole for all the expectations of rescue the men dare cherish. Yet they went on struggling year after year against the handicap of the cold, the long nights, and the absence of all that makes life worth living. Their story is one long testimonial of man's adaptability to environment against heartbreaking odds. For a long time they were without artificial light; then one of them found an area of slimy clay near the centre of the island, and from this modelled with his hands a primitive lamp, which burned animal fat from a wick made of linen. At first there was difficulty with the clay soaking up the fat; then a method of kiln-baking the stuff was devised, and the lamp became an unqualified success—if we may except its incurable way of depositing a film of black, greasy soot on everything around, a little trouble that has been the experience of  every Arctic and Antarctic explorer ever since. When the supply of linen gave out oakum was used as a substitute. As it was, much of their clothing went in supplying the linen for wicks, and the time came when the Crusoe trick of skin clothes had to be resorted to. Reindeer, fox, and bear skins took the place of homespun clothing, bedding, and footwear. The skins were first soaked in water several days until the hair could be pulled off easily. The wet skin was then rubbed with the hands until nearly dry, then smeared over with melted deer fat, which was worked in with the hands until it became soft and pliant. Doubtless it smelled strongly, but from what one knows of the *mujik* that would not trouble him overmuch. For a needle a piece of wire served, and for thread bear and deer sinew.

Slowly, shedding their rotting and worn clothing, the men were metamorphosed into fur-clad Crusoes, but Crusoes of the snows, living exclusively on a meat diet, Crusoes who may never have heard of palms and coconuts.

During the fifth winter on the island one of the men—Feodor Weregin—died, after a lingering illness that had long since rendered him a burden to the other three, who nursed him with the devotion of men who have suffered together. As he died in the winter, when the frozen ground made the

digging of a deep grave a physical impossibility, they buried him as best they could, then knelt on their knees in the dimly lit hut and quaintly prayed that the bears would not come and dig up the body.

On August 15, 1749, more than six years after they had left their ship to explore the island, the three survivors saw a Russian vessel coming into the little harbour. The sight was incredible, for they had long since given up hope of being rescued, and were only convinced that it was not an hallucination when they heard the shouts of the seamen who were putting off in a boat. The captain had come into their bay by a pure coincidence, and had no thought of finding marooned sailors ashore. The vessel belonged to a trader who had intended to winter in Novaya Zemlya, but who, on the advice of the manager of the whaling fishery, changed his plans to winter at West Spitsbergen. The captain had been reluctant to follow the whaling manager's suggestion, and only agreed after some arguments. Had he reached West Spitsbergen the bones of the three men would have been left in the north, but contrary winds drove the ship toward Browne Island, where she hauled up exactly opposite the castaways' beach. Were this coincidence to be made use of in a book of fiction, the censorious reader would damn it as a cheap trick by an unconvincing scribbler. However, there was the ship, and there opposite were three skin-clad

men running about waving their arms and lighting smoke fires on the hills. To make sure of being seen a reindeer skin attached to a pole was swung aloft frantically. But the signals were seen, and the three dirty Crusoes had the exquisite joy of seeing men coming over in a boat.

The manner of their reception on board may have been cordial; we are not told, but we do know that the three men agreed to work for their passage back to Archangel, and pay, besides, eighty roubles on arrival, which may strike some of us as a little grasping on the part of a captain performing an act of mercy. The ship remained in those regions a little longer, and returned to Russia with a rich cargo of deer fat and a great number of bear, fox, deer, and seal skins, a catch which seems to suggest that the little matter of the eighty roubles might have been overlooked. They reached Archangel on September 28 of the same year. The return to civilization was not at first a smooth and easy transition. The austere life of the past six years rendered them impatient of the trivialities and selfishness concomitant with civilization, and, while they gradually came to accept these things, their stomachs never became reaccustomed to spirituous liquor. Nor could they take bread, having been so long without it.

More than a century before the Russian whalemen had been marooned off East Spitsbergen eight Englishmen were left by mischance on the coast of Greenland, where they lived for nine months and twelve days before being rescued. While an exile of three-quarters of a year as an adventure cannot compare with six years, this story of the eight Englishmen is a more living thing, since one of their number, Edward Pelham, gunner's mate, left us such a vivid record that the adventure might have happened yesterday. These men were in the employ of the famous Muscovy Company of Merchant Adventurers, and formed part of the complement of the ship *Salutation*, which had left London on May 1, 1630, for Greenland to hunt the whale, or "sea horse," as Pelham quaintly put it. Our chronicler begins by introducing himself and his seven companions by setting down their names and occupations in this wise:

William Fakeley	Gunner
Edward Pelham	Gunner's mate and chronicler
John Wise	} Seamen
Robert Goodfellow	
Thomas Ayres	Whalecutter [1]
Henry Bett	Cooper
John Dawes	} Landsmen
Richard Kellet	

[1] Called among whalemen the "specksioneer," from the old Dutch word *specksynder—i.e.,* head fat-cutter. The Dutch name is used among the old Nantucket whalemen to this day.

Then follows his preface, which is worth quoting in part, if only for its *naïveté* in comparing their adventure with a similar experience suffered by some Dutch sailors in 1596, to the belittlement of the latter.

Courteous Reader: that *God* may have the only glory of this our Deliverance, give me leave to look back unto that Voyage, which the Dutchmen made into Nova Zembla in the year 1596. In which place, having been (like ourselves) overtaken with the Winter, were there forced to stay it out, as we were. . . . This Nova Zembla stands in the degree 76, North latitude; our Wintering place is in 77 degrees and 40 minutes, that is, almost two degrees nearer the North Pole than they were; and so much therefore the colder. The *Dutch* were furnished with all things necessary both for life and health; had no want of any thing: *Bread, Beer* and *Wine*, they had good and good store. Victuals they had *God's* plenty; and Apparel both for present cloathing, and for shift too: and all this they brought with them in their *Ship. We* (*God* knows) wanted all these. *Bread, Beer* and *Wine* we had none. As for *Meat*, our greatest and chiefest feeding was the *Whale Frittars*, and these mouldy too; the loathsomest meat in the world. For our *Venison*, 'twas hard to find but a great deal harder to get: and for our third sort of Provision, the *Bears*, 'twas a measuring Cast which should be eaten first, we or the Bears, when we first saw one another: and we perceived by them, that they had as good hopes to devour us, as we to kill them.

After making further naïve comparisons with the Dutchmen he concludes:

If therefore the *Dutch* men's Deliverance was worthily accounted a Wonder; ours can amount to little less than a Miracle. The greater therefore our Deliverance, the greater must be *God's* glory: and that's the Author's purpose in publishing it. *God* keep the Reader's from like dangers. So prays he that endured what he here writes of.

EDWARD PELHAM

The *Salutation,* under Captain William Goodler, in company with three other ships, left the Thames with a fair

gale on May 1, as already stated, and arrived at the pre-
determined bay in Greenland on June 11, where they remained for two months while the coopers went ashore to
knock up the oil-casks. On August 15 our eight men were
sent ashore on another part of the coast known as the
Maiden's Paps, with a brace of dogs, three lances, and a
tinder-box, to hunt deer. They reached the shore after four
hours' rowing in fair weather, and before dark had succeeded
in killing fourteen deer. Being too weary from the long pull
to the land followed by the all day's hunting, they agreed
to rest ashore that night and return to the ship the next
morning after further hunting. Eating their small stock of
food, they lay round the camp-fire, and were soon fast
asleep.

In the morning the weather had grown bad; there was
much ice in the offing, and the men had the mortification of
seeing the ship put to sea—a necessary manœuvre in order
to escape being crushed by the incoming floes. As the
weather grew thicker, and the ship was shortly lost sight of,
the men decided, after a discussion, to hunt along the shore
toward Green Harbour, where the other whalers were still
believed to be, and there await the arrival of the *Salutation*.
Working thus toward the determined objective, they succeeded in killing eight more deer, and, with the shallop now
deeply laden, they rowed to Green Harbour, arriving on
August 17, only to find the bay deserted. Puzzled and
worried at this *contretemps*, the men decided to go with all
speed to Bell Sound, sixteen leagues to the south. There
was not a minute to lose, for they knew that only three days
remained before the ships were to leave those waters for that
season. So urgent was the need for haste that the shallop
was lightened by heaving overboard the precious venison.
Sailing and rowing hard, they were half-way to Bell Sound
by nightfall, and, had the night been fine, would have continued the passage, but a fog coming up drove them to
shelter in a cove, where they were kept chafing with im-

patience until noon the following day. Having no compass, and being unfamiliar with the coast, thus rowing and sailing in the dark, Bell Point was overshot by many leagues. Discovering the mistake at daybreak, they put about, and, sailing northward, sighted the summits of lofty mountains which were unrecognized. William Fakeley, the gunner, insisted that they were on the wrong course, and, though opinions were by no means unanimous, the boat's head was once more turned to the south. This was the fatal mistake, for at that time they were within two miles of Bell Sound. Pelham wrote:

> And thus upon the fatal 20th day of August, which was the utmost of our limited time for staying in the country, we again returned quite the contrary way, namely to the Southward. Thus utterly uncertain, when and where to find the Sownd, a thousand sad Imaginations overtook our perplexed minds; all of us assuredly knowing that a million of Miseries would of necessity ensue, if we found not the Ships whereby to save our passage.

Distracted, they turned a second time to the north, the gunner still insisting that they should continue to pursue a southward course. He may have felt that every league to the southward was a league to the good whether the ships were found or not. But, whatever his process of reasoning, he insisted that Bell Harbour lay to the south, and when the others overruled him he refused to steer any longer in protest. The oar was now taken by Pelham. The weather remained good, and, with a fair wind, the shallop made good speed with a sail, and the next day, to the discomfiture of Fakeley, Bell Harbour came in view. With the new day the wind had changed, and now blew a gale off the land, forcing the men to take shelter in a cove two miles from the little harbour proper. Two men were at once sent overland to find out if the ships were still there. The time for their departure had already expired, and the men were not surprised, on arriving at the bay, to find the ships gone. After

learning the depressing truth the little company sadly put
their gear into the boat, and, the sea having moderated,
stood for Bottle Cove in the faint hope that the ships might
be there. Arriving there the next day to be again disappointed, a conference was held to decide what to do,
which way to go. Some still nursed a hope that the ships
would not abandon them, but the more pessimistic, or
realistic, resigned themselves to the worst, and wondered if
it were possible for white men, unprepared, to spend a winter
so far north. To remain at Bell Sound would be suicidal;
the ice was already drifting in; the long Polar winter was
near. No one had ever been known to winter so far north.
They remembered authenticated records of sailors perishing
in the country.

All these fearful Examples, presenting themselves before our
eyes, at this place of *Bottle Cove* aforesaid, made us, like amazed
Men, to stand looking one upon another: all of us, as it were,
beholding in the present, the future Calamities, both in himself
and of his fellows. And thus like Men already metamorphosed into
the Ice of the Country, and already passed both our Senses and
Reason, stood we with the eyes of pity beholding one another.

They lacked provisions, clothing, tents, and other necessities for spending the winter in such a rigorous climate.
Men have been caught in Polar regions before and since, but
seldom, if ever, so poorly equipped for the ordeal.

Thus, for a space standing all mute and silent, weighing with
ourselves the Misery we were already fallen into, and knowing
Delay in these extremities to be the Mother of all Dangers, we
began to conceive Hope even out of the depth of Despair. Rowsing
up our benumbed Senses, therefore, we now lay our Heads and
Counsels together to bethink ourselves of the likeliest course for
our Preservation in that Place; seeing that all hopes of gaining our
Passage into *England* were then quite frustrate.

The upshot of the discussion was a unanimous decision to
make for Green Harbour as soon as the present boisterous

weather abated, and there to hunt and kill venison for the winter. On August 25, the wind being fair, they set sail, and in twelve hours covered the sixteen leagues to Green Harbour. Dragging the shallop ashore, they stretched the sail over the oars, thus forming a crude but serviceable shelter, under which they rested the whole night, and refreshed their bodies with the remainder of the food. The next morning the shallop was rowed two miles along the coast to a spot believed to be overrun with deer. The day's hunting was successful, no less than seven deer and four bears being killed. As the weather had again become threatening the company returned that night to Green Harbour, where a tent was  set up as before with the sail and oars. Before dawn six of the men broke their sleep to go hunting, leaving Fakeley and Dawes in the camp to dress the meat already procured and prepare a meal for the Nimrods' return. Sailing to the previous day's hunting-ground,[1] they espied seven reindeer, and killed six in a short time with the aid of their dogs, and six more during the afternoon.

As it began to rain and blow hard that night, allowing no prospect of hunting for the next few days, it was decided to return to Bell Sound to winter there. Loading the shallop and a small sloop, left at Green Harbour by one of the whale-ships, with bear and deer meat and also a quantity of whale crisp[2] left by the ships after trying out[3] the blubber,

[1] It bore the curious name of Cole's Park.
[2] Crisp, or fritters, is the fibrous membrane left after the rendering of the blubber.
[3] 'Trying out' is the whalemen's name for melting out the blubber.

they prepared to set sail for Bell Sound. But before they could get away it had grown dark, and the company delayed the departure till the Monday, this being Saturday. Sunday was spent mostly in sleeping. Monday morning an early start was made, but after four hours' rowing in the face of a gale they put in at Bottle Cove, allowing the boats to ride at grapnel anchors while the men spent the night ashore. But the wind, blowing hard into the cove, drove the boats on to the rocks, sinking them in shallow water. The meat was found floating in the surf or strewn along the beach. Both boats were, however, saved without serious damage, and on September 3, the weather being fair, the little company succeeded in reaching Bell Sound. Here they found a wooden hut, which they called the Tent, built by Flemish whalemen, and roofed with tiles. Constructed to hold a large number of men, it measured fifty by eighty feet, and was somewhat too roomy for eight men. As the building was too big to keep warm, they tore down a small shack outside, and rebuilt it within the larger structure, partly with bricks from the whalers' try-works.[1] The bricks were firmly cemented with lime found in barrels in the hut and sand from the shore. But so low was the temperature that the mortar had to be kept near a fire to prevent its freezing. While Fakeley and Pelham acted as masons the others helped by mixing mortar and cleaning and carrying bricks.

The little inner house was a sturdy structure, with two sides of boards of double thickness, the intervening space being filled with sand, and the other two sides of brick. A chimney vent, a square tube of wood, let out the smoke into the main hut. The smaller structure measured twenty by sixteen feet by ten feet high, and was perfectly windtight—an important thing in such latitudes. When finished the hut was snug and warm, but as dark as an owl's nest, there being no windows. For light a few tiles were removed from the eaves of the main building, allowing the very

[1] A furnace for boiling out the oil.

doubtful daylight to filter parsimoniously down the wooden chimney. The interior was divided into wooden cabins, each accommodating two men, and with bunks covered with deer-skins. The next care was a fireplace for warmth and for cooking. This was built from one of the broken-down try-works. Of fuel there was no lack in a number of old shallops and oil-casks which lay rotting on the shore.

These were broken up and carried to the hut. Here Edward Pelham feels an explanation and apology is due for breaking up the whaling company's property, pointing out, somewhat unnecessarily, that they had to have this fuel in order to live. But, as in those fine old days 'theft' was punishable by torture or death, the apology and explanation may not be so redundant as it may seem to us.

The weather was now bitterly cold, and the Arctic day-light almost gone. For the next eight months the fire was never allowed to go out. At night it was kept alive by hard-wood embers. On September 12 they saw what are de-scribed as "two sea horses" asleep on an ice floe, and, taking harpoons in a boat, approached within striking distance without waking them. Fakeley harpooned the larger, and the smaller, swimming round the dam, was also dispatched and dragged into the boat before it sank. A week later others were seen out on the floes, dark shapes in the Arctic twilight. But as these were awake the hunters only succeeded in dispatching one of them. Lack of game and the impossibility of returning to hunt at Green Harbour brought to them the necessity of strict economy in food, and it was agreed to have an allowance of no more than one reasonable meal a day, with Wednesdays and Fridays fasting days, except what they could make of whale fritters—a very unattractive diet, with starvation almost a preferable alternative.

By the middle of October the sea had frozen over, and daylight had become almost non-existent. *Ennui* was beginning to take hold of the minds of the men, and every one was seized with uncontrollable moods of black depression. The thought of the approaching long night, when for months they would have nothing to occupy their minds but their own thoughts, filled them with unnamed fears. No work, no hunting, no books — the winter was best not thought about. They often discussed the ship—what had happened to her. Had the captain been a monster of callousness, or had the *Salutation* been lost? The true solution to the mystery—a very simple one—never seemed to have occurred to them.

Another of their fears was the possibility of the wood-supply failing before the winter was over. Against this contingency it was decided to cook half a deer every day, and stow the meat in hogsheads. The whale 'fritters' was already going bad, turning mouldy from the wetting it had received in the sea, and from being closely packed since. Further reduction in rations became necessary when it was found that the bear and venison would not last throughout the winter at the present rate of consumption. From now

on they fed four days a week solely upon whale fritters—
"the loathsomest meat," so wrote Pelham. And, like the
old windjammer sailors who ate their hard tack in the dark
in order that they might not see the weevils in it, these men
found some advantage in consuming their whale fritters
in the gloom of an ill-lit cabin. The sun disappeared on
October 14, and did not return until February 3. Of this
period Pelham picturesquely writes:

> A kind of daylight we had indeed, which glimmered some eight
> hours a day unto us; in October time I mean: for from thence
> unto the first of December, even that light was shortened ten or
> twelve minutes a day constantly. So that from the first of *Decem-*
> *ber*, till the twentieth there appeared no light at all, but all was one
> continued Night. . . . All this darksome time, no certainty could
> we have when it should be Day or when Night; only myself, out
> of my own little judgement, kept the observation of it thus, first
> bearing in mind the number of the Epact: I made my addition
> by a Day supposed, (though not absolutely to be known by reason
> of the Darkness) by which I judged the ages of the Moon; and this
> gave me my rule of the passing of the time. So that at the coming
> of the ships into Port I told them the very day of the Month, as
> directly as they themselves could tell me.

Light was obtained from a lamp made out of a piece of
sheet lead ripped off one of the oil coolers and fed with a
wick from rope yarn suspended in oil. This was kept, like
a Torch of Remembrance, perpetually burning. But it was
a poor glimmer at best, and insufficient to keep away the
hideous depression which sat on their spirits. They moved
about silently in the semi-darkness like dead men, their
mutual interests long since exhausted and hope departed for
ever. Their clothes and shoes were filthy and falling to
pieces, although patched and sewn with rope yarn and canvas. Their faces, feet, and hands were swollen and blistered
by frost-bite as the result of going out for snow or ice for
melting into water. Then at last came the daylight and the
first peep of the sun, which did more than food could do to

revive and hearten the despairing company. Of the wonderful day when they again saw the sun Pelham romantically wrote:

This proved a marvellous cold Day, yet a fair and clear one. About the middle whereof, all clouds now quite dispersed, and Night's sable curtain drawn, *Aurora* with her golden face smiled once again upon us, at her rising out of bed. For now the glorious Sun with his glittering beams began to gild the tops of the lofty Mountains. The brightness of the Sun and the whiteness of the Snow, both together was such, as that it was able to have revived a dying spirit: but to make a new addition to our Joy, we might perceive two Bears, a she one and her cubb, now coming towards our tent.

Armed with nothing but lances, the men, though feeling by no means well, advanced to meet the eager she-bear, who rushed straight at the party and fought savagely against the lethal spears until she lay dead among her exhausted victors. The cub escaped, and the temperature was too low to permit of the ill-equipped hunters venturing far in pursuit. Before the carcass froze stiff it was dragged inside the hut, skinned, and quartered. The meat lasted twenty days and was pronounced good, though after eating the liver the men noticed that much of their skin peeled off—a phenomenon marked by other Polar adventurers. During the following days Bruin came in numbers. Of forty seen twelve were killed, and, with such a larder, food rations were increased to more satisfying proportions. With the return of the sun there need no longer be any fear of a food shortage, and though, paradoxically, the weather seemed as cold as ever, the entire party were feeling the benefits of the sun and sufficient food.

In the middle of March the two dogs (both mastiffs), which had survived the winter, wandered out, and one never returned—either overcome by cold or killed by bears. But now the world was smiling on the forlorn castaways. Setting traps, they caught no less than fifty foxes, and

rarely returned from the daily hunt without a fat bag or a
sack of ducks' eggs. The remaining dog, living so richly,
became fat and lazy, until he would refuse to follow a deer.
On May 25 a strong wind began to break up the sea, and
some of the men climbed a high elevation at the back of the
camp to look out to sea. Hopes of being rescued, which had
fled entirely during the latter days of the winter, had since

returned, and no one would have been surprised to see a
ship come over the horizon.

But when a ship did approach they did not see her, for
they were at prayers in the hut. Thomas Ayres, who had
stepped into the main hut, was the first to sight the ships—
for there were two ships, part of the Hull whaling fleet—
in the little bay. The men at their prayers heard voices
without, and rushed out to find men approaching.

> But we, within, hearing of them, joyfully came out of the tent,
> all black as we were with Smoak, and with our Cloaths all tattered
> with wearing.

The captain of the leading ship knew that the eight men
had been left ashore hereabouts, and had sent men ashore
with orders to search the coast to discover if any of the eight
men were still alive. On seeing the castaways they did not

immediately recognize them as the men left there the year before. Pelham, writing of how they received their rescuers, says:

> Coming thus into us, we shewed them the Courtesie of the House, and gave them such Victuals as we had; which was Venison roasted four Months before, and a cup of cold Water; which, for novelty sake, they kindly accepted of us.

Of their rescuers they demanded news from home, asking endless questions. On board the principal ship they were received with sympathy, and kept until the arrival of the London whaling fleet three days later. After a fortnight of comparatively good food (it was never remarkably good on whalers) and surgical attention they had all fully recovered. Captain William Goodler, the commander of the fleet, gave them clothes " to the value of twenty pounds worth." Four of the men now went aboard their own last year's ship, where their *captain treated them as deserters*! That, then, was his explanation for their marooning. It is difficult to believe that any sane man would choose probable starvation in the Arctic to serving a few months longer on any ship, no matter how hard the life. The ships left Greenland on August 20,

> which day of departure being come, and we embarked, with joyful hearts we set sail through the foaming Ocean; and though crossed sometimes with contrary Winds homeward bound, yet our proper Ships came at last safely to an Anchor in the river of Thames, to our great joy and comfort, and the Merchants benefit.

CHAPTER X

The Distress of Pierre Viaud and his Recovery

IN the year 1766 Lieutenant George Swettenham, on military duty at Fort St Mark in the Appalachian Mountains, interviewed a white man and woman, the survivors of one of the most terrible experiences that has ever been recorded. Afterward, when the man, a Monsieur Viaud, left to return to his own country, the young lieutenant gave him a personal letter to serve him as credentials during his journey. And, since it is meet that the protagonists of these chapters bring with them their credentials (if any), I cannot do better than offer, on behalf of Monsieur Viaud, the letter from Lieutenant Swettenham.

I, the undernamed *George Swettenham*, Lieutenant of the ninth Regiment of Foot, in the Service of His Britannic Majesty, and Commander of the *Fort St Mark*, in the *Appalachian Mountains*, do hereby certify: That on the information of a Savage, who had reported his having met with a dead Body on a Strand, about forty Miles from hence; and having strong reasons to think a Ship had been wrecked on that Coast, which I feared was one that I had expected for some time before, and had received no account of; I detached four Soldiers, with my Interpreter, under the command of *Mr Wright*, Ensign in the same Corps, to visit that Coast, and succour all those he might meet with in any distress.

Mr Wright, on his return, presented the Bearer, *le Sieur Viaud*, and a woman of the same Nation, to me; whom he had found on a desert Coast, in the most deplorable condition, almost famished with hunger: having nothing to subsist on but a few Oysters, and some fragments of a Negro, whom they had been reduced to the necessity of slaying for Food.

Le Sieur Viaud informs me that he is a Sea Captain, and an Officer in the Blues, in the service of the French King; that a Savage he had met with, and who undertook to conduct him to *St Mark*, had robbed him of what Effects he happened to have saved from a Shipwreck, and fled away, during the Night, in his Canoe, leaving him and some other Companions on a desert Island.

Mr Wright, also, presented to me a young man, son of the Woman above mentioned, whom he had found in another desert Island, in a more desperate condition than the former Persons: as it was impossible he could have existed an hour longer without his assistance; having neither Food, nor Sense, nor Motion left, when we found him.

The shocking Situation they were all three in, upon his first meeting with them, their extreme weakness, and some particulars I have since been informed of, from some Savages; sufficiently prove, that the story told me by *le Sieur Viaud*, of his having been pillaged, and betrayed, in the manner above mentioned is true.

On the credit of which, I give this Certificate to the said *Sieur Viaud*, who means to set out for *St Augustine* by the first opportunity, and to go from thence into some of the *French* Colonies.

GEORGE SWETTENHAM

FORT ST MARK
May 12th, 1766

Pierre Viaud sailed from Bordeaux in February 1765 in the ship *L'Aimable Suzette* for San Domingo, in the West Indies, where he arrived safely after an uneventful passage across the Western Ocean. The business which brought him there being quickly completed, Viaud was, within a month, ready to return to France, and though before leaving he fell ill of some island fever he nevertheless insisted on sailing as scheduled. But once at sea his condition grew worse, and the captain of the ship strongly urged him to consent to being put ashore to recover. Viaud agreed to

this, and was landed on the Key of St Louis, where he was
nursed in the house of a compatriot, a Monsieur Desclau,
under whose care he was rapidly restored to health. Though
Viaud was impatient to return to Europe he allowed himself
to be persuaded to join his new friends, headed by Desclau,
in a trading voyage to Louisiana, tempted by tales of vast
profits. A brigantine, the *Tyger*, commanded by a Captain
La Couture, was chartered, and the little company of traders
set sail for the American main on January 2, 1766. All told,
they numbered sixteen people, as follows: Captain La Couture, his wife and small son, MM. Desclau and Viaud, with
the latter's negro slave, the mate, and nine seamen.

Bad weather with contrary winds delayed the voyage from
the start, and after much loss of time a point of land was
sighted, which the captain insisted was Cape San Antonio,
though the others rightly believed it to be the Isle of Pines,
at the western end of Cuba. Viaud, taking a sight, proved
this to be the case, and tried to persuade the captain of his
error, but the latter continued obstinate, and kept to a
course which would and did bring him that night among
the dangerous reefs off the Isle of Pines. The mate being
ill, Viaud was standing his watch when the ship drove among
the rocks in the dark. With great good judgment Viaud,
by tacking about, managed to haul the vessel off, though
she was then leaking dangerously. However, they kept
to sea, and after a trying time, constantly at the pumps,
entered the Gulf of Florida in a dogged attempt to reach
Louisiana before the *Tyger* foundered beneath them. The
hull was by now leaking so badly that no amount of pumping could keep down the flood rising in the hold, and in
order to save the vessel it was agreed to make for the land
with all possible speed. At first the wind was fair for Mobile
harbour,[1] but later it swung round toward Pensacola.[2] But
the winds continued fickle, and for four days they beat about,
seemingly getting nowhere, until the night of February 16,

[1] Alabama.   [2] Florida.

when the ship struck a chain of rocks two leagues off the Florida coast. A heavy wind and sea lifted the vessel off the reef and drove her toward the shore badly damaged aft. The stern-post was smashed and the rudder gone, and the crew were preparing to cut the masts when the brig lay over on her beam-ends, precipitating most of the company into the sea. They were able to climb on to her sides, and in this position they clung precariously

throughout the long night, deluged by rain and terrified by lightning, which crackled into the sea unpleasantly close. At dawn the wretched people saw the land comparatively close, but, owing to the mountainous seas, dared not attempt to reach it. During the day the gale increased, and the position of the shipwrecked people became so desperate that one of the sailors, a Dutchman, let go his hold and attempted to swim ashore. He was drowned in sight of the others. Three of the sailors, undeterred by this tragedy, decided to attempt reaching the shore in a small boat. And though the little craft was rotten and leaking they succeeded in getting safely across. Another terrible night followed for those on the wreck, but at sunrise the next morning the sea had so far moderated that a sailor succeeded in swimming across, carrying rags and handkerchiefs with which to caulk the small boat. Those on the wreck anxiously watched the men ashore busy on the boat, but it was not until three in the afternoon that they were able to launch it. There were eleven people clinging to the side of the wreck, and eight were brought off in the boat in two journeys, the other three getting ashore on part of the stern which had broken away. These were MM. Viaud and Desclau and the negro slave.

That night, after a meagre meal of oysters found on the beach, they slept on the sand. In the morning Dutrouche, the sick mate, died, and was buried in a shallow hole dug with sticks. There was much wreckage on the beach, but little or nothing of immediate use to the castaways. As the sea was now tranquil Viaud rowed out alone to the wreck, which at low tide lay half uncovered. Wading about within the vessel, he was able to collect a miscellaneous lot of stuff —six fusils, a parcel of handkerchiefs, a keg of gunpowder, several blankets, forty pounds of biscuit, and two hatchets. With this treasure he was greeted with joy ashore, and before a camp-fire clothes and blankets were spread out to dry. In a spring of fresh water the hard biscuit was soaked, and, with half a dozen wild fowl (Viaud does not say what species) shot by the best marksman of the company, a satisfying meal was prepared and eaten. Lest they are suspected of the Swiss Family Robinson trick of producing rabbits out of hats, it should be explained that a bag of shot had been found in the wreck.

After a second night *al fresco*, warm and reasonably comfortable round the camp-fire, the little company began to think seriously about the future. They had been wrecked on one of a number of islands which were unlikely to be inhabited, at least by white people. This naturally suggested the thought of Indians. Somewhere in this part of the world dwelt the dreaded Seminole Indians, and from this time onward the castaways lived in fear of being attacked by the red men. And, knowing that the Indians became homicidal maniacs when allowed to get at liquor, all the casks, save three, which were hidden under the sand, were staved as a precautionary measure.

On February 22, the sixth day ashore, the party was awakened by a shout from the seaman on watch, "The savages! We are lost!" This, however, was a slight exaggeration, since the Indians—two men and three woman—were friendly. One of the Indians, who spoke bad Spanish, was able to carry on a halting conversation with one of the sailors who understood that language. After offering small gifts to the white people the Indian who spoke some Spanish explained that he was the chief and that his name was Antonio. They had come to pass the winter on an island three leagues distant, where parts of the wreck had come ashore, tempting them to search the islands for more wreckage. Antonio gave the impression of being a trustworthy fellow, and when he agreed to conduct the party to St Mark, a matter of ten leagues distance, no one doubted but what his motive was one of pure altruism. So, after further talk and protestations of friendship, he departed with his companions in the canoe, taking three sailors with him, and promising to return the next day for the others. And he did return the next day, bringing a bustard and two quarters of a roebuck. After a meal six men, including Pierre Viaud, embarked in Antonio's canoe with some of their effects. Viaud promised to send for the rest at once. On arrival at Antonio's island the three sailors were found safe and well, but the chief now seemed reluctant to return for the five people left behind. It seemed hardly credible that he intended to abandon them in cold blood, yet only after fierce threats could he be made to return to fetch the remaining people. Once they were reunited Viaud reminded Antonio of his promise to conduct them to St Mark, but found him considerably less amiable. The whites were forced, by his suspicious behaviour, to suspect treachery, and kept on their guard, though there was little that they could do. The hotheads were for killing the Indians and taking their canoes, but the more prudent dissuaded them from such murderous intent. Meanwhile Antonio, who had been mysteriously absent for several days, returned, and was bribed to convey the party to the mainland.

On March 5 Captain La Couture, his wife and son, with MM. Viaud and Desclau and the black slave, embarked in one of the canoes, with six pounds of biscuit and the boiled quarters of bear and roebuck as provisions. Antonio and his wife were to act as guides. The eight seamen remained behind with the rest of the savages. The passage, Antonio announced, would require two days. After three leagues he insisted on stopping at an island, where the night was spent. Seven days passed in this manner, stopping at different islands, with no indication of getting any nearer to the mainland. Antonio was definitely under suspicion; his excuses were of the poorest, but he was too crafty to be caught at any roguery, and the whites saw no gain in killing him, as they could easily have done. But this aimless wandering from isle to isle exhausted the company, used up their store of food, and got them nowhere. They were compelled to hunt for oysters on the beaches, and they became so weakened by starvation that they had to spell each other at the paddles at lessening intervals. At last it occurred to Viaud that Antonio meant to wear them all out, and by a process of attrition slowly destroy them. One night he whispered his fears to the others. The former hotheads were in favour of Antonio's instant death, but again they were overruled, while Viaud endeavoured to think out some plan for their safety.

On March 12, after travelling about two leagues, the party landed, utterly exhausted, on yet another island, where they lay round a large fire and fell, supperless, asleep. Viaud dreamed that he saw Antonio sailing away with his wife in the canoe, and woke in alarm at the reality of the dream.

The others saw no omen in the dream, and persuaded Viaud to try to get some sleep. But again the vision returned to him, now so vividly that he got up quietly, and went to look for the canoe. Both it and the Indians had gone! They had taken everything of value, leaving the whites destitute of food and weapons, save a blunt knife Viaud had carried on his person. No use bemoaning their carelessness at allowing such a thing to happen. It *had* happened, and they must face the consequence of their folly with what fortitude they could. Being of Latin temperament, they were inclined at first to give way to despair, but after recovering from the shock the entire party searched the island for anything edible. Meeting with no success, they remembered that a larger island, less than a mile distant and separated by a shallow channel, had fresh water and shellfish, for they had but recently halted there during their crazy wanderings with Antonio. Pressed by hunger, they resolved to venture, sending first the negro, who waded across with a bundle of clothes on his head, and sounding all the way. The rest followed, walking hand in hand over the firm bottom, and reached the other island after one and a half hours in the water. They fell on the sand, seized with cramp after coming ashore, but soon recovered. Their greatest need at this time was a fire, but, having neither flint nor tinder, such a boon was impossible. Though weary to death, hunger drove them forth searching the shore for food until night, when they huddled together for protection against the cold night air, getting up from time to time to stamp about to keep warm. In contrast to the nights the days were scorchingly hot, and the wild sorrel, which was the only thing they could find to eat, did not grow in the shade.

So passed ten days of semi-starvation and physical misery. Then one of the party remembered seeing an old canoe on a neighbouring island which they had visited with Antonio one day. It was separated from their own island by a comparatively narrow channel, but was on the opposite side of their island. Leaving the negro to guard the captain's wife and her son, the others set out the same day, crossing the island after four hours' walking. Wading across with a prayer that the channel might be fordable, they found it necessary to swim the middle stretch, and reached the opposite shore, to fall almost fainting with exhaustion. After recovering somewhat they searched for the canoe, and found it without difficulty. The craft was in a worse condition than they had expected, but they set about repairing it with osiers and moss, working hard till dusk. The prospect of the chilly

night before them and the boon of the smallest piece of flint recalled to Viaud's mind that when they had been here with Antonio the Indian had changed his flint, throwing the old piece away near the camp-fire. As darkness, which falls quickly in those latitudes, was near, the men searched feverishly round the dead embers of the old fire for the flint, and had almost given it up when one of them felt it beneath his foot. For fear of losing the humble flake of stone Viaud carried it in two handkerchiefs round his neck. All the next day they worked on the canoe, caulking its gaping sides with strips from one of the precious blankets, and a sorry-looking basket it made after all their labours.

Viaud and Desclau resolved to make an attempt to reach the eight sailors left with the other Indians by fording the channels, while the captain should endeavour to reach his wife and son. But the channels were too deep and wide for fording, and the two men returned to their own island the next day. They found the others dolefully regarding the canoe. The entire fabric was so rotten that it leaked like a basket, and all their labour seemed entirely wasted. Contemplating a succession of failures, they fell into a deep gloom, which was temporarily forgotten when Viaud stumbled upon the recently dead carcass of a roebuck, which appeared to have been wounded by a hunter and to have bled to death after swimming across to this island. But, whatever the explanation, its meat broiled over the fire made a heartening meal. The men were now impatient to get back to the seamen, and examined the canoe for the twentieth time. Two more blankets were sacrificed to caulk it, and after three days' labour it still spurted water through a hundred cracks. But, growing desperate, they resolved to risk crossing in it to the mainland, a distance of only two leagues, or two miles farther than from Portsmouth to Ryde across the Solent.

It was arranged that the three white men should make the attempt, two to paddle while one baled with his hat. Viaud left his knife and flint with the captain's son, charging him to guard them as he would his life. But when the canoe was launched it began to sink under their weight, and Viaud decided to remain behind. So Desclau and Captain La Couture departed, and were never heard of again. When Viaud returned to the others Madame La Couture, who was seen to be weeping, looked up surprised to see him, but far from displeased. He explained how, as there was not room for all in the boat, he had elected to remain. She listened in silence, and then, to his surprise, gave him to understand how grateful she felt at his remaining with her. For the next few days the four people lived mostly on wild sorrel; the few oysters obtainable could only be reached at low tide. The original company of the *Tyger* was reduced to these four people, assuming that the Indians had contrived the death of the eight sailors left behind. After the captain and Desclau had been gone six days Viaud, concluding that they had perished, conceived the plan of collecting enough wood to make a raft to float them over to the main. This should not be a difficult traverse on a fine day. So hopeful did he become that he regretted not having thought of the idea before so that the others could have assisted. Madame La Couture welcomed the suggestion enthusiastically, and aided Viaud and the negro to collect branches and such tree-trunks as they could lift, while the young boy was employed stripping off the bark. In their weakened state the labour was disheartening, and all had frequently to rest. After the first day's work they were rewarded by finding that the boy had been busy collecting a quantity of shellfish, which had been spread round the fire as for a banquet.

The next day was spent taking the tough rind of the trees and binding the collected wood together to form a crude raft. To make the fastenings more secure they were re-inforced by long strips torn from the remaining blankets. In and out between the longer and more or less parallel pieces of timber were woven small pliant green branches, making, it seemed, a tolerably strong job of the raft. When it was completed a straight sapling was secured upright for a mast, with a red blanket for a sail and unravelled stockings for cordage. As a rudder, a small piece of timber hung out-board aft. Provisioning this ship of hope was a simple matter, with oysters and wild sorrel their only choice. The raft, now completed, only waited for a high tide to float off, and the four people looked forward hopefully to a speedy deliverance.

But Fate had by no means finished playing with them, for that night, the last they expected to spend on the island, a violent storm raised such a sea as to smash the raft to pieces and wash away the pitiful stock of food. The same sea threw up the head and skin of a porpoise, which, though rotten and smelling evilly, the hungry people devoured to the last morsel. For their temerity an hour later all were deadly sick, and for four or five days thereafter suffered from the disgusting disease dysentery. After recovering some-what Viaud and the negro began collecting wood for another raft, while the woman remained with her son, who had not recovered from the fish poisoning. The raft took four days to put together, which brought the date, as near as Viaud could judge, up to April 16. On this day when they went to waken the boy they found him cold as marble—the fire had grown low—and his mother, on seeing him thus, fell into a swoon. But his heart was still beating feebly, and after gently chafing his limbs and body he partially recovered. As both mother and son were now ill, the voyage was postponed, Viaud acting as sick nurse throughout the ensuing night. The boy showed wonderful fortitude, and begged Viaud to take his mother away, saying that he realized that he was dying and only encumbered the others. He was plainly sinking, and Viaud did what he could to comfort him but, with Latin fatalism, the child insisted that his end was near. In the evening he again begged Viaud to take his mother to the mainland. Another storm might come and wreck the raft; there was need for haste, he insisted. His mother, who lay ill out of sight beyond a clump of trees, must be led to believe him already dead. Much drivel is written about heroism, but if this boy's devotion to his mother was not heroic nothing ever was. Viaud, believing him to be *in extremis*, consented at last, and afterward wrote, in describing the parting:

> I gave him a surtout I had on, and my waistcoat, and some shellfish which our negro had collected, dried by the fire, with whatever else I could collect.

He then tried to get some rest, but, being too disturbed in mind and body, sat through the night, talking occasionally with the sick child. At dawn he was barely alive, and Viaud, haggard with fatigue and anxiety, crept away.

When he told the mother that her boy was gone her grief was so terrible that it was some time before she suffered herself to be led to the raft, and Viaud wondered if she would attempt to throw herself in the sea. For a

THE RAFT

change, the day was calm, and the water barely ruffled by the gentle zephyrs, and after a passage that took twelve hours the three people landed on the mainland. It was sunset, and they had come ashore at a place where the sea, overflowing the land, had formed a swamp. The first night was spent on an elevated patch of ground, where they slept round a life-giving fire after a scanty meal of shellfish. But before long they were startled awake by bloodcurdling growls, and saw a bear approaching. Leaping up, Viaud hurled a burning brand at the animal, which kept it from coming nearer. The negro, rendered mad with terror, rushed to a tree, and hauled himself up into its branches, where the bear made an attempt to follow. The negro's cries were almost more bloodcurdling then the growlings of the bear now that the animal had begun to ascend the tree, and though Viaud succeeded in driving Bruin off by hurling flaming brands at it the negro refused to descend till morning. The rest of the night the white man and woman lay on the ground within a ring of burning wood—an effective protection against the most savage of animals. In the morning it was only with difficulty that the negro was persuaded to descend.

The first phase of the tragic odyssey of Pierre Viaud and Mme La Couture had ended, the second and final journey had begun. Of the original sixteen people of the *Tyger*, only three now remained. The Frenchwoman had lost her husband and her beloved son, and there hardly seemed anything left to live for. Yet she did live to go through incredible hardships with the intrepid Viaud, and showed herself to be a woman of unusual courage and resolution. While, as I have suggested, there seemed nothing left for her to live for, if the reader follows the terrible journey to the end it will be found that Mme La Couture's fortitude did indeed earn a splendid reward. Let us go with them into the wilderness and virgin forests that lay between them and final salvation.

The settlement of St Mark lay in an easterly direction, and after they had coaxed the half-crazed negro down from the tree they started off on their trek to civilization. But within half an hour their strength failed, and they were forced to give up any further attempt to proceed that day. After a search for wood the trio lay down within a sort of barricade of branches, where they remained all day, foodless, though they were able to assuage thirst from a pool of muddy water. That night their ring of camp-fires attracted wild beasts, whose roars and howlings caused both the woman and the negro to faint with fear.

In the morning the three wanderers were experiencing the torments of starvation. There was no food to be found in the dry thickets of leafless thorn-bush. The negro seemed to have lost all self-control, for though extremely weak he would climb the trees to eat the leaves. The other two later tried eating some leaves, and in a short time all were seized with terrible griping pains and convulsions. Crawling to the pond, they drank of the muddy water for relief. Now their stomachs swelled, they began vomiting blood, and expected to die. But the next day they were somewhat better, and thereafter rapidly recovered. Around them lay a barren waste, and from a slope of rising ground the sea was seen astonishingly close, thus showing what little progress had been made in the trek toward St Mark. Away to the left lay a vast forest, and at length they made their way toward it. Reaching it, they found it to be a thick jungle, and fell exhausted, so depressed as to feel that at last they had reached the end. This at least were the thoughts of the white man and woman; the negro had long since ceased to think or act rationally.

At this point of his memoirs there enters the first warnings of the unnatural tragedy that was shortly to follow. Lying too exhausted to sleep, Viaud's fevered brain began thinking of how, in circumstances similar to the present one, mariners had cast lots to see who should be sacrificed for the others. He then asks his readers to consider their condition: how despair and the insufferable torments of hunger can affect the mental and moral outlook, and how under such a

strain one may do things that at another time would strike one with horror and loathing; and how, with a well-filled belly, it is quite impossible to think the same as a person starving.

Viaud looks at the negro like a hungry animal, and, indeed, at this moment is nothing more than that. Starvation has impaired his reason and destroyed in an hour the effects of ten thousand years of civilization. The flesh has become paramount, the soul can go to hell so long as the stomach's clamouring may be satisfied. Now we turn to Mme La Couture, *une bonne bourgeoise* of France, and are dismayed to find that she is agitated by the same monstrous desire. Hunger, so incomprehensible to most of us, has metamorphosed these erstwhile good people into fiends. They look at the black slyly, then look at each other, then back to the unwitting negro meaningly. When Viaud looked at her

> she turned her eyes upon the Negro and, pointing to him, cast a look at me so full of horror, as spoke her wishes stronger than Speech could, I seemed to have waited for her encouragement.

Waiting till he is asleep, Viaud murderously strikes the wretched black with a knotted stick, but instead of killing him wakes him up. The poor fellow begs for his life, but it is too late. Viaud has become too frenzied to desist and has turned into a monster. And truth compels us to say that Madame La Couture assists him in the bloody work. The negro is given the *coup de grâce* with a knife in his throat. Dragging the body across the trunk of a fallen tree, they sit down to recover. As reason returned with the calming of their tumultuous hearts, horror filled their souls to the exclusion of all else, and after hastily washing their guilty hands in a pool they fell on their knees and prayed for themselves and their victim. Condemn them if you will, it is not the present chronicler's business to excuse or blame. But the thing was done, and a trembling sinner is more contemptible than a bold one. Possibly the pair went ahead on that principle. At any rate, they lit a fire and began the horrible repast, smoking the quarters and eating large morsels with the unconscious gusto of wild animals.

The next day, greatly strengthened, they resumed the march, carrying, of course, the grisly remains of their humble companion. For several days they journeyed forward through the undergrowth and across swamps, fighting every foot of the way through bulrushes, brambles, thorn, and prickly plants, swollen by mosquito bites and sick with the heat of the sun. To avoid most of these obstacles they turned aside and took to the beach, a decision that might profitably have been made sooner, since there was more like-

lihood of meeting with white people on the coast than in the forests. Having so much recovered from their previous distress, and their minds becoming more normal, they began to be shocked at the thought of eating human flesh. So much so that they would go hungry for a day before bringing themselves to partake of the remains of the negro, which Viaud carried wrapped up in a piece of cloth. One night, when they had set the woods on the coast on fire as a protection against the real and never absent peril from wild beasts, they afterward found two large snakes burnt in the fire, and were glad to cut them up for food, as a change from the human flesh which had become abhorrent. Another day they were fortunate enough to come upon a sleeping crocodile, which Viaud killed by driving a sharp, pointed stake into its throat. The carcass was cut up for food, and the softer part of the skin used for the novel purpose of making into masks, to protect their faces against attacks from mosquitoes.

Once they came to a wide river, and, being too weak to swim across, spent two days walking along its banks to a spot narrow enough to be forded. On this detour Viaud lost his precious flint, a misfortune greater than it may appear. Believing that he had left it at the previous camp, Viaud left Madame La Couture, who was too weak to follow, and retraced his steps back to the old camp, where he arrived that evening. Here he found the flint, and so great was his emotion that he wept for joy. Hurrying back through the forest in the dark, he reached his companion two hours before dawn, and found her terrified of the wild beasts which made the night hideous with their howling.

Each day of the trek was an adventure, an epic struggle against the blind forces of nature. The tale is one harrowing narrative of suffering, of which the foregoing pages have been a fair example. At one river a crude raft was built, on which a successful crossing was made, but not before Viaud's companion had fallen into the water, and had been nearly drowned before she could be dragged out. Of these days Viaud wrote:

> Our Course was soon obstructed by a Wood, choked with strong Reeds and Briars. The Shoes, Buskins and Masks, which we had made with the Cayman's[1] Skin, were worn out, and had melted into pap from their late soaking. Our Bodies were attacked by Mouskitoes, Sandflies and Wasps, against which we had no defence: and the only Provisions we could procure, consisted of the wretched remains of the Negro, and the Cayman.

Now Viaud and the lady changed places: he, exhausted and blind with mosquito bites, lay on the shore absolutely spent, while she prepared a fire and nursed him, even bringing in a tortoise which she had captured. Afterward, while

[1] Crocodile.

she had gone into the woods searching for wild turkeys' eggs, Viaud lay meditating on death, believing his end to be near. For weeks he had fought to keep the woman and himself alive, but nature had beaten him. God help Madame La Couture when he had gone! While lost in these gloomy reflections he is startled by the sound of men's voices, and, peering dimly through his swollen eye-sockets, he makes out a boat and men's forms. He gets to his knees to greet them, but falls forward, and then finds himself being tenderly lifted. The men are Europeans, not savages. They are Englishmen by their speech, and Viaud faints from weakness and emotion. A few drops of some potent liquor revive him. Meanwhile the Englishmen are astonished to see a ragged woman issue from the woods, carrying a wild turkey which she had caught. That night is spent round a vast camp-fire on the beach. The Englishmen are soldiers, and two of their number (one the officer Wright who is mentioned in the letter at the beginning of this narrative) who understand French explain, how they come to be on the coast.[1] Now Viaud, already reviving under their care, is able to tell his story to them in English, having learned this tongue in England, where he had twice been a prisoner of war.

The next morning the two castaways persuaded Ensign Wright to take them in his boat to the island they had quitted, either with the forlorn hope of finding Madame La Couture's boy still alive or, what was more likely, to give the child's body a decent burial. Sailing round the island, they called out every minute or so, but their voices only echoed the mournful silence of the place. Leaving the boy's mother in the boat with some of the soldiers, Viaud went ashore with the young officer and a few men to search for the body. They found it near where the boy had been left dying, now lying face downward as though the little fellow had turned over before breathing his last. The skin was dried in the sun, and the poor child's legs were already

[1] See Lieutenant Swettenham's letter.

covered with loathsome worms. While the soldiers started to dig a grave, Viaud began preparing the emaciated little body for burial.

To his amazement he found on turning the body over that the boy was still alive. Controlling himself, he cautiously poured a few drops of rum between the parched lips, and had the satisfaction of seeing the child's eyes open. Calling the

soldiers to desist in their macabre work, he bade them hasten and fetch the boy's mother. On hearing the news the poor woman became so frantic that it was some time before they dare let her approach her son, lest in her emotional stress she might do him more harm than good. At length Ensign Wright told her that her child had recovered consciousness and was asking for her. When his mother was brought to him he said wearily, still only half in this world, "Where have you been? I have not seen you for many days." The mother's emotion touched the hearts of the rough men, and she was gently drawn away so that they could carry the sick child to the boat, where he was wrapped in clothes willingly offered from the backs of their owners. The night was spent on another island, and the next day the party were astir early to get the boy within reach of medical aid (a poor enough thing those days) as speedily as possible. This day the boy's mind was perfectly clear, and he told them how he had eaten the shellfish and drank the water left with him, and then through weakness had slowly starved. He quite realized that he had not been abandoned in cold blood, and generously remembered that it was he who had begged M. Viaud to take his mother away. This child, sick unto death, had existed from April 19 to May 7—nineteen days alone—while his mother and Viaud, believing him dead, had fought their way through the Florida jungle.

At the fort Madame La Couture was the first to recover her health. For a long time the child lay desperately ill, but, though little hope was entertained for his case, he fully recovered after months of nursing and maternal devotion. And of all that we have read it seems to me that the recovery of the boy is the outstanding and unforgettable feature of this narrative.

What of the eight sailors left behind by Antonio, the Indian? Becoming impatient and suspicious after waiting for a long time, they killed Antonio's relatives in their sleep, and took their canoe. But as there was only room for five in it three men were left behind. These three men were later killed by Antonio, who had returned with a superior force. The five sailors in the canoe were never heard of again. Madame La Couture and her son eventually went to live in her former home in Louisiana. Before leaving she wrote to Viaud expressing her undying gratitude for the part he had played in saving the lives of her son and herself.

As for the protagonist of this strange story, after recovering his health he went to St Augustine by ship, thence to New York, where he arrived in August 1766, and stayed with a French family until the following February, when he sailed for Nantes in command of a French vessel. Arriving at that port after a remarkably good passage of three weeks, he disappeared into the hurly-burly of European life, and, except for the memoirs of his terrible experience, which ran into several editions in France, we hear no more of him.

CHAPTER XI

A Crusoe Miscellany

Now would I give a thousand furlongs of sea for an acre of barren ground; long heath, brown furze, any thing. The wills above be done! but I would fain die a dry death.

WILLIAM SHAKESPEARE, *The Tempest*

GONZALO'S preference for a dry death is understandable. Between the barren rock and the deep sea is a poor choice, but faced with it there is no hesitation. Richard Falconer preferred his hump of sand and an existence of almost unprintable beastliness to a watery oblivion—as would most of us when it came to the point.

Casting the mind back over these tales of Crusoes, the salient point of them all is the extraordinary amount of suffering humans will endure if only they may be allowed to live. Physical torture, cannibalism, madness, degradation—any or all of these, it would seem, are worth the price of being allowed to live. It is curious, but the reason lies too deep within the primitive hearts of us to be easily explained, unless by that inconclusive word 'instinct.' If men fight to obtain the best seats at a spectacle, if they rush and push toward the exits of a burning theatre, they are monsters of selfishness and cowardice; but if they will suffer any indignity and beastliness, such as Falconer assuaging his thirst with urine and Viaud killing the negro for his flesh, they are regarded as something in the nature of supermen. They have endured, fought, and lived. It is as though we still rated the animal qualities in ourselves higher than those less tangible qualities to which the soul of man aspires.

However, in this concluding chapter we will not harrow our feelings with further revolting episodes that have darkened some of the foregoing narratives. I intend to narrate briefly a number of castaway experiences in widely scattered parts of the world. Some of these tales have been set down in other books of mine, otherwise they would have had whole chapters to themselves. And, though repetition is a bad thing, there are exceptions to the rule—for instance, when we are the losers by adhering to it.

Down in the Southern Indian Ocean, to the south and east of the Cape of Good Hope, lies a number of lonely islands and mere rocks that have been the scenes of many tragic shipwrecks. There have been survivors, otherwise their stories would not have become known, but, on the other hand, there must have been many unsung Crusoes who have all perished without the world knowing their fate.

Most people have heard of the albatross which was found some years ago on the beach near Fremantle, Australia, with a tin band round its neck, on which were punched the words in French: "Thirteen castaways have taken refuge on the Crozet Isles. Help, for the love of God!" and how they were never found.

It was on such an isolated rock that the East Indiaman *Doddington* left the survivors of her company in July 1755. She left the Downs on April 23 in convoy with four other ships, but, being a faster sailer, risked prowling corsairs and forged ahead, reaching the Cape in seven weeks, after a brief call at Boavista, Cape Verde Islands. On July 5 she doubled the Cape, and ran due east for twenty-four hours between latitudes 35° 30' and 36°, then altered course to east-north-east, which course she kept for twelve days, when an untimely rock brought the voyage to a sudden and tragic conclusion. She struck between one and two bells in the middle watch,[1] and at once began to pound so violently that there was no standing on her decks. The *Doddington* carried 270 people, passengers and crew, *of whom only twenty-three got ashore alive*, these being all men. Captain Samson was among the drowned. Those to get ashore were the first officer, Evans Jones, second, third, and fifth officers, John Cottes, William Webb, and S. Powell, also the carpenter, two quartermasters, the captain's steward, the surgeon's servant, two other servants (one coloured), eleven seamen, and a midshipman.

Though dazed by their buffeting and the suddenness of the catastrophe they had the presence of mind to search among the rocks for whatever useful stores and wreckage might be washed up. Their second care was to try to produce a fire to dry their sodden clothing. An attempt by rubbing sticks together failed, but when a box containing two gun-flints and a broken file was found a fire was started by striking the spark into some gunpowder bruised on a piece of linen. This gunpowder was obtained from a keg-full, mostly wet, but dry in the centre. As there appeared to be nothing whatever on the rock, the necessity of salvaging stores from the wreck was impressed upon every one. The first stores to come ashore were a box of wax candles and a case of brandy, and from the latter every one had a dram as a stimulant. Shortly afterward a cask of fresh water was found undamaged, and then a few pieces of nasty grey pork. Casks of flour and other stuff could be seen farther out beyond reach, spilled out of the ship like apples from a burst basket.

As night approached a tent of sailcloth was erected on the highest spot, as a precaution against the unknown tides. A

---

[1] Between 12.30 and 1 A.M.

great number of sea fowl hovered about, which explained the heavy deposit of guano which covered the rock to the depth of a foot. The first night was spent miserably, a rain and wind putting the fire out, and sleep made impossible from cold and hunger. Next morning a search for provisions was prosecuted vigorously. The casks seen the previous day lay smashed on the rocks, but a cask of flour and another of beer were intact. After these had been dragged up with considerable labour the incoming tide prevented further salvage. The first food for twenty-four hours, a few scraps of boiled pork, was shared out and eaten between groans of despair from the faint-hearts. Amid these lamentations some one suggested that, as the carpenter had been spared, he might be able to build a boat from the wreckage if tools could be found. Chips, who from this point on became the centre of interest, declared that a boat could certainly be built if wood and tools were at hand. Now the more feckless changed their mood, for, regarding the boat already half built, they forgot their repining, as children laugh before their tears are dry. The matter of starvation, which hung over them like the shadow of death, was quite forgotten in the excitement of planning the boat.

They fell to debating the size it should be, and what point to make for—the Cape or Delagoa Bay. After dinner, while some mended the tent, which had become torn, others searched the rocks, but without success.

The next day, which was Saturday, was a more lucky one. No less than four casks of water, one of flour, and one of brandy were washed up. One of the boats, a small craft, not large enough to carry the entire company, and badly battered, was thrown ashore. There were still no tools except a scraper, not a very valuable implement as such.

The next day a tremendous surf rolled in, throwing up heavy objects which, besides ship's timbers, included a rather useless chest of specie, and a box whose contents were priceless, for in it was found two quadrants, an azimuth compass card, a chisel, a small adze, a file, gimlets, sail-needles, and three sword blades. One of the searchers came upon the  body of a woman, who, by her dress, was recognized as the wife of the second mate John Cottes. As he had not seen it some of the others engaged his attention on the opposite side of the rock while a grave was dug and the corpse buried, the funeral service being read from a French prayer-book that had been picked up. Not until some days afterward was the second mate shown the grave, and given the little wedding-ring from the dead woman's finger. At first the poor man broke down, and afterward spent several days raising a monument with the squarest stones he could find, after which he put up an elm plank on which was inscribed her name, age, and the date of her death, along with a brief account of the disaster.

On July 21 casks of water and pork as well as timber,

canvas, and cordage were washed up. But the carpenter still lacked sufficient tools. He had made a saw, but had neither hammer nor nails. About this time a Swedish seaman named Hendrick Scantz, who had once been a smith, picked up a damaged pair of bellows, and informed Chips that if he would help him (Scantz) to construct a forge he could make nails from old iron burnt out of the wood. Three days were occupied in mending the bellows and building a primitive forge. For an anvil the ring and nut of the bower anchor were made to serve. A thirty-foot sloop with a twelve-foot beam was decided upon, and on July 27 the carpenter and one of the quartermasters laid down the keel at a spot suitable for launching. With his forge and 'anvil' the ingenious Swede made a hammer and a number of nails. After a week on the boat the carpenter became ill, and his condition was anxiously watched until he was able to return to work a few days later.

As the food was now nearly exhausted every one agreed to rations being reduced to two ounces of bread a day. The salt pork was being saved for the boat journey. There were also some live hogs that had been washed ashore, but these were being kept as long as possible. Driven by their need, more determined efforts were made to secure food, and it was found that by a little patience the gannets could be knocked down, though their flesh was rank and "black as a sloe." A catamaran, from which to fish, was made, and three seals were caught, but for some reason or other all who ate of their flesh were sick. On August 20 the midshipman, out fishing on the raft, was blown out to sea, and would have perished but for the carpenter's hastily patching the small boat and putting off for the boy. Though the craft leaked dangerously he managed to reach him and bring the raft back. Afterward Chips repaired the boat so that it could be safely used for fishing, though their piscatorial efforts met with no reward. An attempt was made to preserve from putrefaction the carcasses of the gannets killed, but without success. Sometimes these birds would come in clouds; at other times there would not be one in sight. The efforts to cure the flesh had been to boil them with salt in a copper pan made by the smith, but the result gave every one verdigris poisoning, which brought on violent retching.

On September 3 they had been on the rock seven weeks, and had once during this time seen a column of smoke

toward the west which would indicate that the African coast could not be far distant. Being impatient to get away, a quartermaster, Bothwell, and two seamen, Rosenburg and Taylor, set out in the small boat with a tiny ration of food and water. Meanwhile the building of the sloop proceeded as rapidly as possible, but was interrupted for a short time by what might have been a fatal accident, for the carpenter cut his leg with the adze, and nearly bled to death before the hæmorrhage could be stopped. The return of the small boat from the mainland was awaited eagerly. One day the look-out came running with the news that he had seen the boat, but with only one man in it. As it drew closer another man, who had been bending down, was seen to rise from the bottom of the boat. On landing the pair were found to be Rosenburg and Taylor. They fell on their knees and

thanked God for their deliverance, but were too exhausted to
tell their story until refreshed with food and water. Then
they were allowed to fall asleep without being questioned.
When they awoke they related a dreadful tale to the others.
Land had been found six leagues distant. In the high surf
the boat was overset, and Bothwell was drowned. The
others got ashore exhausted. Of their food and stores only
a small keg of brandy was saved. They lay on the sand till
the next day, too weak to haul up the overturned boat. On
the beach they found the body of Bothwell horribly muti-
lated by some prowling animal. Unable to face the thought
of another night on shore, the two men resolved to return
without reconnoitring the terrain. But a westerly gale prevented a start that day, and the night was spent under the
boat. The next morning they were found by some natives,
whom they called Indians, though they were described as
having woolly hair and black skins. These amiable savages
robbed the white men, and, after doing some damage to the
boat to obtain the iron in it, let them go. That was their
story, hardly an encouraging tale for men who proposed to
land on that inhospitable shore.

On Sunday, September 29, after morning prayers, it was
discovered that the chest of specie had been broken open
and most of the treasure taken. The officers proposed to
write out an oath of denial to be solemnly signed by all those
who were innocent of the theft, but the seamen refused to
enter such a compact, and the matter was dropped. It was
known that the seamen would not regard the taking of the
treasure as a theft, for they believed that all wreckage was
common property. After the loss of the ship they would
lose their pay, and a belief that the officers would have in any
case monopolized the specie relieved them of any compunc-
tions in taking it.

A week later a fowling-piece was picked up, albeit with
the barrel badly twisted. But, being of soft iron, it was not
difficult to straighten, and later was of great use in bringing

down gannets, which flew over in such clouds that it was impossible to miss them. On October 20 the second and third mates and two seamen, out on the raft fishing, were driven outside the rocks, and had to spend the night on a rock among a family of seals. November, December, and January passed without incident. At last, in the middle of February 1756, the sloop was launched, and christened *Happy Deliverance*. Two days later the party of men left the rock, which they had named Bird Island, for good. The boat carried six kegs of water, two hogs which had been kept alive all those months, about ninety pounds of biscuit, and ten days' rations of half-rotten salt meat.

A course was set for Santa Lucia, on the Natal coast, but the wind being foul they stood for the Cape of Good Hope. On March 10 they dropped anchor off an unknown shore. The natives, however, were friendly, and the white men stayed with them two weeks before proceeding northward. Santa Lucia was reached on April 6, and the Delagoa river on April 20. Here their odyssey ends.

In the *Geographical Magazine* for August 1874, in Part III of the *Voyage of the Challenger* by Captain J. E. Davis, R.N., is a most interesting description of the finding of the two German brothers who had voluntarily settled on the lonely Inaccessible Island of the Tristan da Cunha group in the South Atlantic.[1] At New Edinburgh, the little settlement on Tristan, the *Challenger's* people first heard of the two Crusoes. I quote from the *Geographical Magazine*:

Captain Nares was informed by the inhabitants that nearly two years before two Germans had landed on Inaccessible Island—one of the three islands of the group, about twenty miles to the southwest of Tristan da Cunha—and as no communication had taken place between the two islands for a long time it was doubtful if they were in existence. This information induced Captain Nares to visit the island, and, leaving the anchorage at 4 P.M., at 10 they

---

[1] A brief account of the adventure is given in *The Atlantic*, by the present author.

stopped off Inaccessible Island. The next morning, being off the
east side of the island, a hut was observed on the beach, and a boat
sent in. As she approached the two Germans were seen standing
on the beach, a little to the northward of the hut, evidently hesi-
tating as to what they should do. As all men act who for a long
time have existed without intercourse with their fellow-creatures,
they seemed to doubt whether their visitors were disposed to be
friendly, but they were seen to walk towards the boat, and gladly
accepted a passage to the Cape of Good Hope. The story of their
long sojourn on the island, although it reads like another of Defoe's
tales, has the advantage over *Robinson Crusoe* that it is substantially
true in every particular. It seems that the younger of the two
Germans, Gustav Stoltenhoff by name, had been a seaman in the
ship *Beacon Light* in 1870, and when on a voyage from Scotland to
Rangoon the ship had caught fire when between 600 and 700 miles
from Tristan da Cunha. She had steered for the island, and the
fire kept under for three days, but on the evening of the third day
the hatches were blown off, and as the ship was no longer tenable
the captain and crew were obliged to take to the only remaining
boat, and, with a small supply of provisions and water, started to
make their way to the island, then considered three hundred miles
distant; but it is supposed they must have been much nearer than
that, as, two days after, they made the peak of Tristan da Cunha,
and, being seen from the island, a boat went to their assistance,
and they were taken in tow to the island, where they were kindly
received by the inhabitants. Eighteen days later they were taken
off by another ship and landed at Aden. From Aden young Gustav
Stoltenhoff made his way back to the Fatherland—only to find the
family ruined by the Franco-German war, his brother, who had
served in it, a beggar without occupation.

Young Gustav remembered the care-free days at Tristan
da Cunha, where there were no laws, no wars, no taxes, and
no worries, and proposed to his elder brother that they
should migrate there, giving him such rosy descriptions of
the island that the brother agreed. Being poor, they worked
their way to St Helena, from whence a passage was taken to
Tristan da Cunha in a whaler. At St Helena they spent their
small savings on an outfit which included an old whaleboat

picked up cheaply. In November 1871 they embarked at
St Helena on the Yankee whaler *Java*, Captain Mander.
During the passage the captain persuaded them to settle
on Inaccessible Island,[1] which he described as fertile and
abounding in wild pigs and goats. They were landed there
on November 27, with their old boat and stores consisting of
rice, flour, biscuits, sugar, tea, coffee, salt, pepper, tobacco,
a small supply of wine and spirits, matches, oil, powder and
shot. They also brought a lamp, rifle, fowling-piece, tools,
cooking utensils, wheelbarrow, garden seeds, seed potatoes,
empty barrels, and for companionship a dog and pups,
and a library of ten books, which they got to know by heart
after a few months. They landed on a shingle beach on the
western side opposite a ravine, which gave a difficult access
to the tableland at the top of the cliffs. Four days after they
had landed a party of sixteen men arrived in two boats from
Tristan. Their manner was friendly, and they pointed out
to the brothers that they had chosen an exposed position
facing the prevailing north-west winds, and helped them
move their stores to a more sheltered spot. They also gave
useful assistance in building a stone hut, after which they
departed, promising to return at Christmas.

The two Crusoes quickly settled down to their lonely life,
clearing a patch of ground, planting seed, and gathering
wood. By the aid of the long grass they climbed to the
summit of the cliff, where they found four miles of broken,
uneven ground. This month (November) was the pupping
season for the seals, which used the island as a *pied-à-terre*,

[1] The Tristan da Cunha group consists of the Tristan da Cunha, Nightingale,
and Inaccessible Islands, and lies midway between South America and the Cape of
Good Hope in 37° 5′ South and 12° 16′ West, which means about 2000 miles from
Cape Town and 4000 miles from the Horn. The nearest port, Jamestown, St Helena,
lies 1500 miles to the north-east. Tristan is the only inhabited island. Here
lies a small community of semi-literate people, descendants of soldiers and sailors
who have been wrecked or voluntarily settled there, and both coloured and white
women. About 1880 the population reached 109, but dwindled later, through various
causes. In 1885 a tragedy took fifteen of the strongest men, who were drowned
in a lifeboat while going out to provision a calling ship. The census in 1925 gave
130 inhabitants.

and from the boat nineteen seals were caught, though for some reason they were unable to render the blubber. Much amusement was got from watching the mother seals teaching their babies to swim. While sealing the boat, being too heavy for two men to handle, was damaged so badly that it became unsafe to use it.

THE "SEA CART"

In April, the next year, the tussock grass on the cliff-face caught fire, making it no longer possible to reach the plateau by the cliff. The only alternative was round by sea, but because of the accident to the boat the brothers found themselves marooned on their beach. Undaunted, they cut the whale-boat in two, and boarded up the end of the better half, which was dubbed the *Sea Cart*. With this curious vessel they were able to get round the coast to a point from which the summit of the island could be reached. Here were pigs and goats in plenty, and the goat flesh was found

235

particularly agreeable, but the pigs' flesh, owing, it was believed, to the animals' carnivorous habits, was unpleasant when cooked. On May 14 an English ship was sighted, and a beacon fire was lighted. The captain afterward reported the seeing of the signals to the Tristan colony, but the sea ran too high to make it safe to land. The winter's heavy gales had begun, and the Crusoes were by no means happy.

This month they suffered a serious misfortune in the loss of the boat, which was smashed on the rocks. The stores were running low; and though there were plenty of fish out in the deeper water there was no boat with which to reach them.

In the middle of August a colony of penguins arrived to prepare their nests, and in September the females laid their eggs, an act which saved the brothers' lives, as their food was entirely gone when the egg-laying so providentially began. This month a French ship called, and the captain gave them half a hundredweight of biscuit in exchange for a quantity of penguins' eggs, but he could spare no other stores. In October the sealing schooner *Themis* called, leaving a small quantity of pork and tobacco, the captain promising to return a few weeks later, though he never appeared again. At the end of October the penguin eggs failed. A week later the pork and biscuits gave out, and the brothers decided that they must swim round the bluff to gain the land above. Powder and matches were towed behind in a sealed cask. But so precipitous were these shores that it was not until the next day that they reached the tableland. Here they remained, living on wild goat and pig, until December 10, sleeping at night in a rude stone shelter. To this their dreams of an island sanctuary had come. In December a Yankee whaling schooner called, but the brothers declined the offer to be taken off, as they believed that the *Themis* would return as promised. After the schooner had departed a party of the Tristan men landed, and killed forty seals besides shooting nearly all the remaining goats, after which they left. Though now sick and weary of the unequal struggle the two brothers did not ask to return with the Tristan men, fearing that they were no longer welcome among them.

In January Frederic, the elder brother, swam alone round the bluff and climbed to the plateau. Here he shot four pigs, and threw them down to the brother below. There were still four goats on the island, but early in February the Tristaners came again and shot the remaining four. Their present conduct was difficult to understand in the face of their former friendliness, but the brothers concluded that the men wished to drive them from the island. Frederic remained several days on the plateau before rejoining his brother. In March the food being again exhausted made another visit to the plateau necessary. Tobacco, their one comfort, had long since failed. They still had their three dogs, but they were shot, for one day they broke loose and caused such havoc among the penguins that it was suspected they were mad.

The food problem had now become so desperate that the pair decided to separate, one living on the plateau solely to hunt. After many vicissitudes during a month's separation Frederic rejoined his brother, but not before he was nearly drowned while swimming round the bluff. In June he again went to the plateau, where he remained until August 18. The last three months they had lived solely on swine's flesh. The *Challenger's* arrival on October 16 terminated their privations and their island dreams.

Lying in the Pacific some hundreds of miles to the south of New Zealand are the Auckland Islands, which have been the temporary refuge of more than one party of unwilling Crusoes. The islands are bleak, uninhabited, and sparsely covered with tussock grass and stunted, wind-blown trees. So common are wrecks on these shores that the New Zealand Government has erected a shed on the larger island, housing a boat, a store of food, blankets, and clothes. Also a relief steamer, the *Hinemoa*, calls periodically. In *The Pacific* I have related the adventures of the shipwrecked crews of the schooner *Grafton* and the barque *Dundonald* on the Aucklands, but as both narratives are germane to our subject I shall retell them briefly here.

On January 2, 1864, the schooner *Grafton*, of Sydney, Captain Musgrave, having left that port some months previously on a sealing voyage, ran into a heavy gale when off the entrance to Carnley Harbour, at the southern end of Auckland Island, and, in spite of the drag of two anchors, drove on a lee-shore. The crew — the captain, Mr Raynal the mate, and three men — saved their lives, but little else. When the weather moderated they were able to get a few stores from the wreck, and built themselves a hut from wreckage, thatching the roof with the only plentiful thing on the island—tussock grass. Here they began a Crusoe-like existence, gradually making their abode more comfortable with rude chairs, bunks, and a table. A fireplace was built of unmortared stones with a chimney of tin, copper, and zinc salved from the schooner.

The men were at first greatly alarmed by the sea-lions, which came at night close up to the camp, barking like dogs; but it was found that they could be easily dispatched. Once, however, a large 'tiger' sea-lion attacked one of the men so ferociously that the fellow was obliged to escape by climbing a tree. Here he was kept prisoner until the infuriated animal was killed by the rest of the party.

They made themselves clothing, hats, and foot-gear from the skins of the seal. Like Crusoe, they went clothed in skins. How often has this useful little animal been the means of saving life in the bleak places of the earth! Another Crusoe touch is provided by a parrot which they taught to talk. The discovery of a  parrot with a nest of young birds in these latitudes (where the winter is severe) was astonishing, but one young bird, which they caught and tamed, thrived well despite the climate.

Before they had been long on the island the castaways discovered it to be the home of a number of wild dogs, whose barking had been at first confused with that of the sea-lions. They resembled sheep dogs, and were concluded to be descendants of dogs left by some ship. They lived in burrows like wild cats, but one was caught and domesticated without difficulty. The daily fare of the castaways was seal, boiled

239

or roast, and fried roots, but we hear no complaints of this hardly Lucullian fare. But, however philosophical their dispositions, they were of no mind to remain in this bleak country for ever. So work was begun on a boat, built from the hull of the schooner, whose bones still lay wedged among the rocks near the beach. But, owing to the lack of proper tools, the job proved impossible, and was abandoned. Some one thought of lengthening their small, twelve-foot boat,

and this plan was carried out, though the result was anything but reassuring, for the craft looked as if it would fall apart with the least motion. But, as food had all but gone and the men were at the point of starvation, three of them, the captain, the mate, and one seaman, decided to risk putting to sea in her, leaving the other two behind at their own request. The three men departed on July 19, 1865, and after a passage of six terrible days reached Stewart Island, New Zealand, after a Crusoe existence lasting eighteen months. The other two men were picked up by a schooner sent out from Stewart Island to get them.

Some months after the *Grafton* was wrecked on the southernmost extremity of Auckland Island a large square-rigger, the *Invercauld*, Captain Dalgarns, Melbourne for Callao, was thrown ashore on the northern coast, six out of her company of twenty-five men being drowned. The others, including Captain Dalgarns and his first officer, got safely ashore. They had landed practically without food, and suffered torments from starvation. As the months passed the men died of scurvy one by one, until there were only three left alive, the captain, the mate, and one seaman. They too would have soon died but for the timely coming of a Portuguese ship, the *Julian*, from Macao for Callao, with coolies. The *Julian* had developed a leak, and, seeing a light ashore, the captain had sent a boat to see if he could secure assistance.

The experience of the survivors of the four-masted barque *Dundonald* is a more contemporary matter, since their Crusoe adventure occurred in the year 1907. The *Dundonald*, with a crew of twenty-eight, left Sydney on February 18 for Falmouth with wheat. As soon as she was clear of the Heads she ran into bad weather, which was the cause of her piling up on Auckland Island seventeen days later. Shortly after striking the rocks at the foot of soaring cliffs she went down, taking her skipper, Captain Thorburn, his sixteen-year-old son, and a number of the crew with her. More were drowned in an attempt to reach the cliff. The survivors, sixteen altogether, got ashore by scrambling along the mizen topsail-yard, which touched the rocks. The half-clad, bare-footed men ran about to keep warm, and then searched the coast for the depot of stores they knew existed on one of the islands. They were on Disappointment Island, which did not, however, possess a depot of this kind. The cold rain and piercing winds made some sort of shelter imperative, and to that end a seaman was lowered over the cliff to the jigger mast to secure the gaff topsail. Raising a wall of peat sods, they stretched the canvas over it, thus forming a rough shelter, under which the survivors lay shivering, until one of the men discovered a few matches in his pocket. After a few days' illness the mate died on March 18, and was buried in the peat on the hillside.

The ship had disappeared, leaving only her wrecked spars sticking out of the sea. Nothing but the piece of canvas and a few sticks of wood had been saved, hence the marooned men were less fortunate than most castaways, who, as a rule, manage to save something—a little food, a gun, and a boat maybe. To make their position more wretched winter was approaching, and their camp site was exposed to biting winds. Driven by cold from the hillside, they searched for, and found, a more sheltered spot, a hollow on the opposite side of the island. Here with sticks they dug out holes six feet square and as many deep, over which were laid poles covered with twigs and grass sods. In these troglodyte dwellings they lived for months, secure against the wind if not always against the rain, which had a way of penetrating the flat roofs. I have omitted to provide our men with food, but there is no producing rabbits from hats here. The first days they had subsisted on molly-hawks' eggs, but later they were able to knock down the birds themselves, and, as their hunting abilities improved, they were able to catch the lordly albatross and an occasional seal. Five underground houses were built, and before each a fire was lighted, and not allowed to go out during the seven months on the island.

The manner of their living, how necessity turned the seamen to ingenious makeshifts, is unusually interesting. Without tools they had built themselves houses; now their thoughts turned toward a boat of some sort, for a larger

IN THE MIZEN-TOP

island in the offing tempted them to try to reach it before winter arrived. It was now July, and flurries of snow gave warning of what was to come. Two of the seamen began collecting pieces of gnarled scrub, until they had enough to 'weave'—one can think of no better word—a coracle-like vessel. Over this canvas was tightly stretched, and sewn with thread pulled from the canvas and needles made from birds' wing-bones. These often broke, and the work was dishearteningly slow. Paddles were fashioned out of forked branches covered with canvas. Only July 31 two men set out for the larger island and were gone twelve days. They reported having seen wild pig but no food depot. As the birds were departing and food growing more difficult to obtain, it was decided to construct more boats to transfer the entire party across to the larger island. Two more of these craft were finished after a month's patient work, but one was smashed in the surf on the first attempt to launch it. In the other the third mate and one seaman got away without mishap, and landed on the island the same night. In getting through the breakers the boat was upset and wrecked, but, what was more serious, the live embers, which they had brought across in a stone 'stove' were quenched, and they came ashore cold and wet without means of making a fire. Wandering along the shore, they came upon a board on a post, bearing the grand words "Four miles to depot along the beach." Hurrying forward, they reached the hut at dusk, and found not only a boat there, but food, clothes, blankets, and firearms. For three days they were held back by the weather, but as soon as possible returned to their companions and brought them over. The men had been seven and a half months on Disappointment Island. A flagstaff, on which was hoisted a white flag, was erected to attract passing ships, and this flag and one of the coracle boats is now in the museum at Christchurch, New Zealand. Early in November the relief steamer *Hinemoa* arrived on her periodical call, and picked up the survivors.

A notorious place for wrecks is the group of islands in
the Southern Indian Ocean known as the Crozets. Like
the Aucklands, they seem to have a sinister attraction for
sailing-ships. They consist of two groups: Inaccessible,
Hog, Possession, and East Islands, and the Twelve Apostles.
They are treeless rocks, rising to a height of 5000 feet, and,
owing to their isolated position and inhospitable character
—there are no beaches—they are seldom visited by ships.
Possession Island is the largest of the group. The nearest
continent is Africa, 2000 miles to the north-west.

The most famous castaways on the Crozets, and therefore
too well known to require more than passing mention here,
were the forty-nine survivors of the square-rigged ship
Strathmore,[1] which was wrecked on one of the Twelve
Apostles in the early morning of July 1, 1875. After cruel
hardships, during which a few of their number died, their
signals were seen by an American whaler, the *Young Phœnix*,
and they were taken off after spending nearly seven months
on the rock.

Two other victims of the notorious Crozets were the
sealing vessels *Princess of Wales* and *Adventure*, which were
wrecked there within five years of each other—that is, in the
years 1820 and 1825. The first victim was the *Princess of
Wales*, cutter, with a crew of fifteen men who had gone
expressly to the Crozets, where at certain seasons seals
were known to be plentiful. But, instead of staying a few
weeks, the loss of the cutter on the treacherous lee-shore
left them marooned, to be picked up nearly two years afterward by the American sealer *Philo*.

The *Adventure*, a fifty-five-ton schooner, also out for seals,
left her bones there in the summer of 1825. Her crew of
sixteen men spent eighteen terrible months on the islands [2]
before they were found and brought back by Captain
Duncan, of the whaler *Cape Packet*. The captain confessed

[1] The story is told in *Ships and Sailors*, by the present author.
[2] Nine men had got ashore on one island and seven on another some distance off.

that he had never even heard of these islands before, and had stumbled on them, as it were, by the merest chance.

Rivals to the Crozets in the competition for transient guests are the two islands of St Paul and Amsterdam, which lie some sixty miles apart in the middle of the Southern Indian Ocean, just half-way between Tasmania and Cape Town, on approximately the 38th parallel. St Paul Island, the southernmost, is simply the crater of an extinct volcano, with a segment of its giant rim broken down and allowing a view of the interior of the crater from the sea. (St Paul Island is not to be confused with St Paul's Rocks in the South Atlantic.) Both islands belong to France, though Amsterdam, as its name suggests, was discovered by a Dutchman—the famous navigator Anthony van Diemen.

In August 1853 the new 600-ton barque *Meridian*, with 84 passengers, including 41 children, and a crew of 22, went ashore in the dark on Amsterdam Island. Though the entire company of 106 people got ashore alive they were permitted to escape with no more than their lives, and would assuredly have starved to death had they not been quickly rescued.[1] But after ten days of suffering, especially for the children, the American whaler *Monmouth*, attracted by the red-shirt flag on a pole, sent boats ashore and took every one off. Three weeks later they were landed at Mauritius, whence the Governor sent them to their various destinations, after £1200 had been publicly subscribed for their benefit.

In the middle of the month of June 1871 the Government transport *Megæra*, overcrowded with troops for Australia, ran into a hurricane when somewhere near the island of St Paul. The *Megæra*, an old iron vessel, began to leak so badly that it was found impossible to check the inpouring water. A diver who had gone over the side to examine the hull reported that a knife could be pushed through her corroded plating! When it was seen that the ship could not

[1] Another account says that the captain and two men were lost. See *The Indian Ocean*, by the present author.

float much longer she was run inshore on St Paul, where most of the stores were landed. They found there two Frenchmen in charge of tents and equipment for the summer whalers, whose voluntary Crusoedom would automatically terminate with the arrival of the whalers. Their island solitude was suddenly broken by the arrival of several hundred uninvited guests, but as these guests had brought ample stores there was no severe hardship for anyone during their three months' stay. They were found and taken off by two ships, the P. and O. steamer *Malacca* and H.M.S. *Rinaldo*, that arrived within a day of each other at the end of August.

As recently as the winter of 1931 St Paul [1] again appeared in the news as the scene of a castaway drama. In 1928 some Frenchmen promoted a company to start a lobster fishery on the island and erect there a canning factory. Experts in lobster fishing and canning from Brittany were sent out to begin fishing and erect a factory, but from the start they were dogged with difficulties, until misfortune reached its climax in a severe earthquake and fire which destroyed the factory and brought the venture to an unexpected end. The greater part of the company's employees was brought back to France in March 1930, but the manager and his wife (M. and Mme Brunon) and five men volunteered to remain on the island to look after the stores and machinery until a ship could be sent to take it off. But the relief vessel, a small, under-powered steamer, was delayed by a long series of gales, while the seven people meanwhile suffered frightful privations. A baby was born to the manager's wife, but, owing to her own state of health and the lack of proper medical attention, the infant died within a few days. To make matters worse for the harassed manager, sickness broke out among the men, some of whom went mad and died from exposure. The first to succumb was a negro called François,

[1] The island has since been reported completely swallowed up by the sea (not an unknown happening with volcanic isles), though I have no means of confirming this report.

who crawled out of the hut to the top of rock, where he shortly afterward died. The corpse was quickly converted to a skeleton by the carnivorous sea birds. A few days after the negro had crawled away to die another man, M. Pulloch, died. The next was M. Brunon, who died while in his

wife's arms. A fourth member of the little group, Pierre Quillivic, a Breton like most of the others, donned his beloved Breton costume, and taking his dory,[1] paddled out to sea and never returned. Whether he was deranged, or had some idea of going for help, will never be known. Food was almost gone, the survivors were starving and all down with scurvy, and, as one of those rescued, a Monsieur Le

Huledet, afterward said, had not some of the party died they would have all starved to death, since there was not enough food for every one. Then it is possible that Pierre Quillivic, like Captain Oates, made the supreme sacrifice in the hopes of saving the lives of his companions. Madame Brunon, a native of Concarneau, in Brittany, was the heroine of the tragedy. In spite of sickness and an injured foot which prevented her from stirring out of the hut for nearly a month, she nursed her husband after having so shortly before gone through the ordeal of childbirth.

When the relief ship approached the island her people could see the smoke from the burning volcanic hills, and as

[1] A small boat peculiar to Brittany and the North Atlantic coast of America.

they drew nearer they could make out two or three forlorn figures watching them from the cliffs, where they had watched the sea for weeks past. They were in a wretched plight from scurvy and starvation, and in a few more days would have died, but for the eleventh-hour rescue.

And now, reader, we will go our different ways. The Crusoes and castaways we have adventured with are but a moiety of that vast company who have tasted the pleasures and horrors of solitude and privation. The time must come when such experiences are no longer possible—the time, not perhaps far distant, when the isolated places are no longer isolated: when the world is shrunk to insignificant proportions by the linking up of its remotest parts through aerial transportation, wireless, television, and heaven knows what other mechanical wizardry. Then St Paul, the Crozets, the Aucklands, and even the Poles themselves will be week-end resorts, with canned music, condensed food, and all the comforts of home. When that time comes the drama enacted on St Paul Island in the year of grace 1931 will be regarded as fantastic as Crusoe's experience may seem to us.

INDEX

INDEX

253

INDEX

Wase, Captain, 60
Webb, William, 226
Weregin, Feodor, 180, 186
Weymouth, H.M.S., 55
White, Richard, 67
Wilkins, Peter, 31
Woodes Rogers, Captain, 39, 46, 47, 51, 56, 57

Wyss, Johann David, 35

YAHOOS, 35
York, 18
Young Phœnix, whaler, 245
Youwarkee, 31
Yucatan, 60, 70

A CATALOG OF SELECTED
DOVER BOOKS
IN ALL FIELDS OF INTEREST

A CATALOG OF SELECTED DOVER BOOKS IN ALL FIELDS OF INTEREST

100 BEST-LOVED POEMS, Edited by Philip Smith. "The Passionate Shepherd to His Love," "Shall I compare thee to a summer's day?" "Death, be not proud," "The Raven," "The Road Not Taken," plus works by Blake, Wordsworth, Byron, Shelley, Keats, many others. 96pp. 5 3/16 x 8 1/4. 0-486-28553-7

100 SMALL HOUSES OF THE THIRTIES, Brown-Blodgett Company. Exterior photographs and floor plans for 100 charming structures. Illustrations of models accompanied by descriptions of interiors, color schemes, closet space, and other amenities. 200 illustrations. 112pp. 8 3/8 x 11. 0-486-44131-8

1000 TURN-OF-THE-CENTURY HOUSES: With Illustrations and Floor Plans, Herbert C. Chivers. Reproduced from a rare edition, this showcase of homes ranges from cottages and bungalows to sprawling mansions. Each house is meticulously illustrated and accompanied by complete floor plans. 256pp. 9 3/8 x 12 1/4. 0-486-45596-3

101 GREAT AMERICAN POEMS, Edited by The American Poetry & Literacy Project. Rich treasury of verse from the 19th and 20th centuries includes works by Edgar Allan Poe, Robert Frost, Walt Whitman, Langston Hughes, Emily Dickinson, T. S. Eliot, other notables. 96pp. 5 3/16 x 8 1/4. 0-486-40158-8

101 GREAT SAMURAI PRINTS, Utagawa Kuniyoshi. Kuniyoshi was a master of the warrior woodblock print — and these 18th-century illustrations represent the pinnacle of his craft. Full-color portraits of renowned Japanese samurais pulse with movement, passion, and remarkably fine detail. 112pp. 8 3/8 x 11. 0-486-46523-3

ABC OF BALLET, Janet Grosser. Clearly worded, abundantly illustrated little guide defines basic ballet-related terms: arabesque, battement, pas de chat, relevé, sissonne, many others. Pronunciation guide included. Excellent primer. 48pp. 4 3/16 x 5 3/4. 0-486-40871-X

ACCESSORIES OF DRESS: An Illustrated Encyclopedia, Katherine Lester and Bess Viola Oerke. Illustrations of hats, veils, wigs, cravats, shawls, shoes, gloves, and other accessories enhance an engaging commentary that reveals the humor and charm of the many-sided story of accessorized apparel. 644 figures and 59 plates. 608pp. 6 1/8 x 9 1/4. 0-486-43378-1

ADVENTURES OF HUCKLEBERRY FINN, Mark Twain. Join Huck and Jim as their boyhood adventures along the Mississippi River lead them into a world of excitement, danger, and self-discovery. Humorous narrative, lyrical descriptions of the Mississippi valley, and memorable characters. 224pp. 5 3/16 x 8 1/4. 0-486-28061-6

ALICE STARMORE'S BOOK OF FAIR ISLE KNITTING, Alice Starmore. A noted designer from the region of Scotland's Fair Isle explores the history and techniques of this distinctive, stranded-color knitting style and provides copious illustrated instructions for 14 original knitwear designs. 208pp. 8 3/8 x 10 7/8. 0-486-47218-3

Browse over 9,000 books at www.doverpublications.com

ALICE'S ADVENTURES IN WONDERLAND, Lewis Carroll. Beloved classic about a little girl lost in a topsy-turvy land and her encounters with the White Rabbit, March Hare, Mad Hatter, Cheshire Cat, and other delightfully improbable characters. 42 illustrations by Sir John Tenniel. 96pp. 5³⁄₁₆ x 8¼. 0-486-27543-4

AMERICA'S LIGHTHOUSES: An Illustrated History, Francis Ross Holland. Profusely illustrated fact-filled survey of American lighthouses since 1716. Over 200 stations — East, Gulf, and West coasts, Great Lakes, Hawaii, Alaska, Puerto Rico, the Virgin Islands, and the Mississippi and St. Lawrence Rivers. 240pp. 8 x 10¾.
0-486-25576-X

AN ENCYCLOPEDIA OF THE VIOLIN, Alberto Bachmann. Translated by Frederick H. Martens. Introduction by Eugene Ysaye. First published in 1925, this renowned reference remains unsurpassed as a source of essential information, from construction and evolution to repertoire and technique. Includes a glossary and 73 illustrations. 496pp. 6⅛ x 9¼. 0-486-46618-3

ANIMALS: 1,419 Copyright-Free Illustrations of Mammals, Birds, Fish, Insects, etc., Selected by Jim Harter. Selected for its visual impact and ease of use, this outstanding collection of wood engravings presents over 1,000 species of animals in extremely lifelike poses. Includes mammals, birds, reptiles, amphibians, fish, insects, and other invertebrates. 284pp. 9 x 12. 0-486-23766-4

THE ANNALS, Tacitus. Translated by Alfred John Church and William Jackson Brodribb. This vital chronicle of Imperial Rome, written by the era's great historian, spans A.D. 14-68 and paints incisive psychological portraits of major figures, from Tiberius to Nero. 416pp. 5³⁄₁₆ x 8¼. 0-486-45236-0

ANTIGONE, Sophocles. Filled with passionate speeches and sensitive probing of moral and philosophical issues, this powerful and often-performed Greek drama reveals the grim fate that befalls the children of Oedipus. Footnotes. 64pp. 5³⁄₁₆ x 8 ¼. 0-486-27804-2

ART DECO DECORATIVE PATTERNS IN FULL COLOR, Christian Stoll. Reprinted from a rare 1910 portfolio, 160 sensuous and exotic images depict a breathtaking array of florals, geometrics, and abstracts — all elegant in their stark simplicity. 64pp. 8⅜ x 11. 0-486-44862-2

THE ARTHUR RACKHAM TREASURY: 86 Full-Color Illustrations, Arthur Rackham. Selected and Edited by Jeff A. Menges. A stunning treasury of 86 full-page plates span the famed English artist's career, from *Rip Van Winkle* (1905) to masterworks such as *Undine, A Midsummer Night's Dream,* and *Wind in the Willows* (1939). 96pp. 8⅜ x 11.
0-486-44685-9

THE AUTHENTIC GILBERT & SULLIVAN SONGBOOK, W. S. Gilbert and A. S. Sullivan. The most comprehensive collection available, this songbook includes selections from every one of Gilbert and Sullivan's light operas. Ninety-two numbers are presented uncut and unedited, and in their original keys. 410pp. 9 x 12.
0-486-23482-7

THE AWAKENING, Kate Chopin. First published in 1899, this controversial novel of a New Orleans wife's search for love outside a stifling marriage shocked readers. Today, it remains a first-rate narrative with superb characterization. New introductory Note. 128pp. 5³⁄₁₆ x 8¼. 0-486-27786-0

BASIC DRAWING, Louis Priscilla. Beginning with perspective, this commonsense manual progresses to the figure in movement, light and shade, anatomy, drapery, composition, trees and landscape, and outdoor sketching. Black-and-white illustrations throughout. 128pp. 8⅜ x 11. 0-486-45815-6

THE BATTLES THAT CHANGED HISTORY, Fletcher Pratt. Historian profiles 16 crucial conflicts, ancient to modern, that changed the course of Western civilization. Gripping accounts of battles led by Alexander the Great, Joan of Arc, Ulysses S. Grant, other commanders. 27 maps. 352pp. 5⅜ x 8½.   0-486-41129-X

BEETHOVEN'S LETTERS, Ludwig van Beethoven. Edited by Dr. A. C. Kalischer. Features 457 letters to fellow musicians, friends, greats, patrons, and literary men. Reveals musical thoughts, quirks of personality, insights, and daily events. Includes 15 plates. 410pp. 5⅜ x 8½.   0-486-22769-3

BERNICE BOBS HER HAIR AND OTHER STORIES, F. Scott Fitzgerald. This brilliant anthology includes 6 of Fitzgerald's most popular stories: "The Diamond as Big as the Ritz," the title tale, "The Offshore Pirate," "The Ice Palace," "The Jelly Bean," and "May Day." 176pp. 5⅜ x 8½.   0-486-47049-0

BESLER'S BOOK OF FLOWERS AND PLANTS: 73 Full-Color Plates from Hortus Eystettensis, 1613, Basilius Besler. Here is a selection of magnificent plates from the *Hortus Eystettensis,* which vividly illustrated and identified the plants, flowers, and trees that thrived in the legendary German garden at Eichstätt. 80pp. 8⅜ x 11.
0-486-46005-3

THE BOOK OF KELLS, Edited by Blanche Cirker. Painstakingly reproduced from a rare facsimile edition, this volume contains full-page decorations, portraits, illustrations, plus a sampling of textual leaves with exquisite calligraphy and ornamentation. 32 full-color illustrations. 32pp. 9⅜ x 12¼.   0-486-24345-1

THE BOOK OF THE CROSSBOW: With an Additional Section on Catapults and Other Siege Engines, Ralph Payne-Gallwey. Fascinating study traces history and use of crossbow as military and sporting weapon, from Middle Ages to modern times. Also covers related weapons: balistas, catapults, Turkish bows, more. Over 240 illustrations. 400pp. 7¼ x 10⅛.   0-486-28720-3

THE BUNGALOW BOOK: Floor Plans and Photos of 112 Houses, 1910, Henry L. Wilson. Here are 112 of the most popular and economic blueprints of the early 20th century — plus an illustration or photograph of each completed house. A wonderful time capsule that still offers a wealth of valuable insights. 160pp. 8⅜ x 11.
0-486-45104-6

THE CALL OF THE WILD, Jack London. A classic novel of adventure, drawn from London's own experiences as a Klondike adventurer, relating the story of a heroic dog caught in the brutal life of the Alaska Gold Rush. Note. 64pp. 5³⁄₁₆ x 8¼.
0-486-26472-6

CANDIDE, Voltaire. Edited by Francois-Marie Arouet. One of the world's great satires since its first publication in 1759. Witty, caustic skewering of romance, science, philosophy, religion, government — nearly all human ideals and institutions. 112pp. 5³⁄₁₆ x 8¼.   0-486-26689-3

CELEBRATED IN THEIR TIME: Photographic Portraits from the George Grantham Bain Collection, Edited by Amy Pastan. With an Introduction by Michael Carlebach. Remarkable portrait gallery features 112 rare images of Albert Einstein, Charlie Chaplin, the Wright Brothers, Henry Ford, and other luminaries from the worlds of politics, art, entertainment, and industry. 128pp. 8⅜ x 11.   0-486-46754-6

CHARIOTS FOR APOLLO: The NASA History of Manned Lunar Spacecraft to 1969, Courtney G. Brooks, James M. Grimwood, and Loyd S. Swenson, Jr. This illustrated history by a trio of experts is the definitive reference on the Apollo spacecraft and lunar modules. It traces the vehicles' design, development, and operation in space. More than 100 photographs and illustrations. 576pp. 6¾ x 9¼. 0-486-46756-2

A CHRISTMAS CAROL, Charles Dickens. This engrossing tale relates Ebenezer Scrooge's ghostly journeys through Christmases past, present, and future and his ultimate transformation from a harsh and grasping old miser to a charitable and compassionate human being. 80pp. 5³⁄₁₆ x 8¼. 0-486-26865-9

COMMON SENSE, Thomas Paine. First published in January of 1776, this highly influential landmark document clearly and persuasively argued for American separation from Great Britain and paved the way for the Declaration of Independence. 64pp. 5³⁄₁₆ x 8¼. 0-486-29602-4

THE COMPLETE SHORT STORIES OF OSCAR WILDE, Oscar Wilde. Complete texts of "The Happy Prince and Other Tales," "A House of Pomegranates," "Lord Arthur Savile's Crime and Other Stories," "Poems in Prose," and "The Portrait of Mr. W. H." 208pp. 5³⁄₁₆ x 8¼. 0-486-45216-6

COMPLETE SONNETS, William Shakespeare. Over 150 exquisite poems deal with love, friendship, the tyranny of time, beauty's evanescence, death, and other themes in language of remarkable power, precision, and beauty. Glossary of archaic terms. 80pp. 5³⁄₁₆ x 8¼. 0-486-26686-9

THE COUNT OF MONTE CRISTO: Abridged Edition, Alexandre Dumas. Falsely accused of treason, Edmond Dantès is imprisoned in the bleak Chateau d'If. After a hair-raising escape, he launches an elaborate plot to extract a bitter revenge against those who betrayed him. 448pp. 5³⁄₁₆ x 8¼. 0-486-45643-9

CRAFTSMAN BUNGALOWS: Designs from the Pacific Northwest, Yoho & Merritt. This reprint of a rare catalog, showcasing the charming simplicity and cozy style of Craftsman bungalows, is filled with photos of completed homes, plus floor plans and estimated costs. An indispensable resource for architects, historians, and illustrators. 112pp. 10 x 7. 0-486-46875-5

CRAFTSMAN BUNGALOWS: 59 Homes from "The Craftsman," Edited by Gustav Stickley. Best and most attractive designs from Arts and Crafts Movement publication — 1903–1916 — includes sketches, photographs of homes, floor plans, descriptive text. 128pp. 8¼ x 11. 0-486-25829-7

CRIME AND PUNISHMENT, Fyodor Dostoyevsky. Translated by Constance Garnett. Supreme masterpiece tells the story of Raskolnikov, a student tormented by his own thoughts after he murders an old woman. Overwhelmed by guilt and terror, he confesses and goes to prison. 480pp. 5³⁄₁₆ x 8¼. 0-486-41587-2

THE DECLARATION OF INDEPENDENCE AND OTHER GREAT DOCUMENTS OF AMERICAN HISTORY: 1775-1865, Edited by John Grafton. Thirteen compelling and influential documents: Henry's "Give Me Liberty or Give Me Death," Declaration of Independence, The Constitution, Washington's First Inaugural Address, The Monroe Doctrine, The Emancipation Proclamation, Gettysburg Address, more. 64pp. 5³⁄₁₆ x 8¼. 0-486-41124-9

THE DESERT AND THE SOWN: Travels in Palestine and Syria, Gertrude Bell. "The female Lawrence of Arabia," Gertrude Bell wrote captivating, perceptive accounts of her travels in the Middle East. This intriguing narrative, accompanied by 160 photos, traces her 1905 sojourn in Lebanon, Syria, and Palestine. 368pp. 5⅜ x 8½. 0-486-46876-3

A DOLL'S HOUSE, Henrik Ibsen. Ibsen's best-known play displays his genius for realistic prose drama. An expression of women's rights, the play climaxes when the central character, Nora, rejects a smothering marriage and life in "a doll's house." 80pp. 5³⁄₁₆ x 8¼. 0-486-27062-9

CATALOG OF DOVER BOOKS

DOOMED SHIPS: Great Ocean Liner Disasters, William H. Miller, Jr. Nearly 200 photographs, many from private collections, highlight tales of some of the vessels whose pleasure cruises ended in catastrophe: the *Morro Castle, Normandie, Andrea Doria, Europa,* and many others. 128pp. 8⅞ x 11¾. 0-486-45366-9

THE DORÉ BIBLE ILLUSTRATIONS, Gustave Doré. Detailed plates from the Bible: the Creation scenes, Adam and Eve, horrifying visions of the Flood, the battle sequences with their monumental crowds, depictions of the life of Jesus, 241 plates in all. 241pp. 9 x 12. 0-486-23004-X

DRAWING DRAPERY FROM HEAD TO TOE, Cliff Young. Expert guidance on how to draw shirts, pants, skirts, gloves, hats, and coats on the human figure, including folds in relation to the body, pull and crush, action folds, creases, more. Over 200 drawings. 48pp. 8¼ x 11. 0-486-45591-2

DUBLINERS, James Joyce. A fine and accessible introduction to the work of one of the 20th century's most influential writers, this collection features 15 tales, including a masterpiece of the short-story genre, "The Dead." 160pp. 5³⁄₁₆ x 8¼. 0-486-26870-5

EASY-TO-MAKE POP-UPS, Joan Irvine. Illustrated by Barbara Reid. Dozens of wonderful ideas for three-dimensional paper fun — from holiday greeting cards with moving parts to a pop-up menagerie. Easy-to-follow, illustrated instructions for more than 30 projects. 299 black-and-white illustrations. 96pp. 8⅜ x 11. 0-486-44622-0

EASY-TO-MAKE STORYBOOK DOLLS: A "Novel" Approach to Cloth Dollmaking, Sherralyn St. Clair. Favorite fictional characters come alive in this unique beginner's dollmaking guide. Includes patterns for Pollyanna, Dorothy from *The Wonderful Wizard of Oz,* Mary of *The Secret Garden,* plus easy-to-follow instructions, 263 black-and-white illustrations, and an 8-page color insert. 112pp. 8¼ x 11. 0-486-47360-0

EINSTEIN'S ESSAYS IN SCIENCE, Albert Einstein. Speeches and essays in accessible, everyday language profile influential physicists such as Niels Bohr and Isaac Newton. They also explore areas of physics to which the author made major contributions. 128pp. 5 x 8. 0-486-47011-3

EL DORADO: Further Adventures of the Scarlet Pimpernel, Baroness Orczy. A popular sequel to *The Scarlet Pimpernel,* this suspenseful story recounts the Pimpernel's attempts to rescue the Dauphin from imprisonment during the French Revolution. An irresistible blend of intrigue, period detail, and vibrant characterizations. 352pp. 5³⁄₁₆ x 8¼. 0-486-44026-5

ELEGANT SMALL HOMES OF THE TWENTIES: 99 Designs from a Competition, Chicago Tribune. Nearly 100 designs for five- and six-room houses feature New England and Southern colonials, Normandy cottages, stately Italianate dwellings, and other fascinating snapshots of American domestic architecture of the 1920s. 112pp. 9 x 12. 0-486-46910-7

THE ELEMENTS OF STYLE: The Original Edition, William Strunk, Jr. This is the book that generations of writers have relied upon for timeless advice on grammar, diction, syntax, and other essentials. In concise terms, it identifies the principal requirements of proper style and common errors. 64pp. 5⅜ x 8½. 0-486-44798-7

THE ELUSIVE PIMPERNEL, Baroness Orczy. Robespierre's revolutionaries find their wicked schemes thwarted by the heroic Pimpernel — Sir Percival Blakeney. In this thrilling sequel, Chauvelin devises a plot to eliminate the Pimpernel and his wife. 272pp. 5³⁄₁₆ x 8¼. 0-486-45464-9

Browse over 9,000 books at www.doverpublications.com

AN ENCYCLOPEDIA OF BATTLES: Accounts of Over 1,560 Battles from 1479 B.C. to the Present, David Eggenberger. Essential details of every major battle in recorded history from the first battle of Megiddo in 1479 B.C. to Grenada in 1984. List of battle maps. 99 illustrations. 544pp. 6½ x 9¼. 0-486-24913-1

ENCYCLOPEDIA OF EMBROIDERY STITCHES, INCLUDING CREWEL, Marion Nichols. Precise explanations and instructions, clearly illustrated, on how to work chain, back, cross, knotted, woven stitches, and many more — 178 in all, including Cable Outline, Whipped Satin, and Eyelet Buttonhole. Over 1400 illustrations. 219pp. 8⅜ x 11¼. 0-486-22929-7

ENTER JEEVES: 15 Early Stories, P. G. Wodehouse. Splendid collection contains first 8 stories featuring Bertie Wooster, the deliciously dim aristocrat and Jeeves, his brainy, imperturbable manservant. Also, the complete Reggie Pepper (Bertie's prototype) series. 288pp. 5⅜ x 8½. 0-486-29717-9

ERIC SLOANE'S AMERICA: Paintings in Oil, Michael Wigley. With a Foreword by Mimi Sloane. Eric Sloane's evocative oils of America's landscape and material culture shimmer with immense historical and nostalgic appeal. This original hardcover collection gathers nearly a hundred of his finest paintings, with subjects ranging from New England to the American Southwest. 128pp. 10⅝ x 9. 0-486-46525-X

ETHAN FROME, Edith Wharton. Classic story of wasted lives, set against a bleak New England background. Superbly delineated characters in a hauntingly grim tale of thwarted love. Considered by many to be Wharton's masterpiece. 96pp. 5 3/16 x 8 ¼. 0-486-26690-7

THE EVERLASTING MAN, G. K. Chesterton. Chesterton's view of Christianity — as a blend of philosophy and mythology, satisfying intellect and spirit — applies to his brilliant book, which appeals to readers' heads as well as their hearts. 288pp. 5⅜ x 8½. 0-486-46036-3

THE FIELD AND FOREST HANDY BOOK, Daniel Beard. Written by a co-founder of the Boy Scouts, this appealing guide offers illustrated instructions for building kites, birdhouses, boats, igloos, and other fun projects, plus numerous helpful tips for campers. 448pp. 5 3/16 x 8¼. 0-486-46191-2

FINDING YOUR WAY WITHOUT MAP OR COMPASS, Harold Gatty. Useful, instructive manual shows would-be explorers, hikers, bikers, scouts, sailors, and survivalists how to find their way outdoors by observing animals, weather patterns, shifting sands, and other elements of nature. 288pp. 5⅜ x 8½. 0-486-40613-X

FIRST FRENCH READER: A Beginner's Dual-Language Book, Edited and Translated by Stanley Appelbaum. This anthology introduces 50 legendary writers — Voltaire, Balzac, Baudelaire, Proust, more — through passages from *The Red and the Black, Les Misérables, Madame Bovary,* and other classics. Original French text plus English translation on facing pages. 240pp. 5⅜ x 8½. 0-486-46178-5

FIRST GERMAN READER: A Beginner's Dual-Language Book, Edited by Harry Steinhauer. Specially chosen for their power to evoke German life and culture, these short, simple readings include poems, stories, essays, and anecdotes by Goethe, Hesse, Heine, Schiller, and others. 224pp. 5⅜ x 8½. 0-486-46179-3

FIRST SPANISH READER: A Beginner's Dual-Language Book, Angel Flores. Delightful stories, other material based on works of Don Juan Manuel, Luis Taboada, Ricardo Palma, other noted writers. Complete faithful English translations on facing pages. Exercises. 176pp. 5⅜ x 8½. 0-486-25810-6

Browse over 9,000 books at www.doverpublications.com